Also by Barbara Hoi

MATH ALIENS, COME – I NEED YOU!
Unlock the Math Genie in a Fun and Creative Way
(Available soon)

How to help your Dyslexic Child to Master Arithmetic

THE RIGHT BRAIN FOR THE RIGHT TIME

Unlock the Dyslexic Potential and
Transform from a Frustrated Reader to
an Inspiring Leader

Barbara Hoi

"The Right Brain for the Right Time"
- ISBN-13: 978-1490916620
ISBN-10: 1490916628, title IB 4349979

Published in November 2013

Davis Dyslexia Correction®, Davis Orientation Counseling®, Davis Math Mastery®, Davis Symbol
Mastery®, Davis ADD Mastery ™, Davis Learning Strategies®, the DDAI logo, and the name Davis™
are trademarks of Ronald D. Davis and Davis Dyslexia Association International.

Visit our website:
At: www.sydneydyslexia.com
Or: www.autismsydney.com

Contact the author on: hoi.barbara1@gmail.com

Thank You

To Keanu, the reason for this book
To Bianca, for inspiring and organising me
To Dean, for endless support and wisdom
To Ben, for his gentle kindness
To Josef, the love of my life
To all my clients for what they taught me

CONTENTS

ABOUT THIS BOOK

- You don't have to be Dyslexic, but it helps. -

The world is speeding up. Weeks are flying by, information flooding us, technology submerging our lives—fast and increasingly visual.

Dyslexics are picture thinkers. They fit perfectly into this new world of infinite possibilities, intuitively aware of their potential.

Given the right tools to harness the power of their right brain thinking, dyslexics can use creativity to focus and tap into the universal mind to re-define themselves.

This is an exciting time if you know how to participate as a conscious creator, and none are better equipped for it than those who are currently struggling in our schools: our picture thinkers. If you are lucky, you too are one of them.

The author shows insights, methods and ways for parents to help their children unlock their vast potential and turn their difficulties into assets, opening new pathways to learning that they can use at school and in life. The book is equally useful for dyslexic adults, who are ready to confront their weaknesses and upgrade their perception, mind and learning strategies.

The wheels of change are turning fast. Many of society's organisations are on the brink of breaking apart, our education system being one of them. Many students, teachers, parents and educators agree on this— yet reality hasn't caught up to that realisation and, as a result, many students still feel like prisoners in this outmoded system.

I've read somewhere recently that anyone being sent back to our present time, having lived on Planet Earth one hundred years ago, would only recognise one institution, one pillar of our society that hasn't radically changed—and that would be our school system.

Without the power to influence the structure of schools, nor the method of teaching, we have to find a way to empower the individual. Children who don't fit the box—and they arrive in increasing numbers—need to be taught how to harness their creativity, visual talents and problem solving skills to overcome the challenges.

If not, we will end up losing a large percentage of future talent, and they will lose the confidence—or ability—to willingly contribute to society.

This book will look at ways to provide some insights and tips, based on the age and ability of a child or adult. It may help a frustrated mother or teacher to better understand those they love and care for, but often cannot reach or help. It will reassure a dyslexic adult that it is never too late to learn and process new information—to be and to become anything they set their mind to. In order to re-shape that mindset, all our human qualities have to be aligned: our body and our emotions, mind and spirit.

Did you know that 46% of Australians don't have the literacy skills to participate effectively in present day Australia?

Did you know that 17% of Australians are illiterate or very poor readers, being on band 1 of a 5-band-literacy scale?

Did you know that there is a $200 per week income difference between level 1 and level 2 readers?

Imagine if there was a way to empower a non-reader to unlock a potential they have always known to be present but are unable to tap into. Imagine the impact this can have on any individual's life, the choices they make, the professions they choose, the circle of friends and, most of all, their self-confidence. Imagine how this would also affect our economy and society at large.

These figures by the Australian Bureau of Statistics in 2007 were reached by testing Australian adults from different levels of education, background, socio-economic groups and races, asking people to read literature relevant in modern society: workplace agreements, leases and newspaper articles. Despite this rather poor outcome, Australia's literacy levels are comparatively high. In 2003 it ranked number 4 on the Pisa* Ranking—unfortunately it has now dropped in the ranking to 9th place for literacy. The PISA results show comparisons in Reading, Maths and Science of 15-year-olds from over **70 countries.**

Would you like to know if dyslexia could be holding you back?
Do you know what you are really capable of?
*PISA - Programme for International Student Assessment

3

The Right Brain for the Right Time

FOREWORD

Everyone sees dyslexia as a disease or a dysfunction. Yet, for me, I believe it's an evolutionary process that humanity is growing toward, and that everyone will have more right-brain function than left-brain function sometime in the future. Dyslexia is that move from left brain to right brain.

There is a very interesting woman on TedTalks called Jill Bolte Taylor, a brain scientist, who had a stroke. She describes her experience in the midst of this stroke, where her left brain shut down and her right brain took over and she had this amazing experience of total connection with the universe and she was able to discern things and have an experience we would not normally have—and it is because of being entirely connected to her right brain she saw her entire experience in the midst of this stroke. It's our left brain that keeps us separated from the reality of the universe. Our right brain experiences the reality of the universe. We block it out—our logic says, "NO, this can't be true."

What's required in the future is an evolutionary process where we connect more and more to our right brain experience. The reason for that is that we have moved from an agricultural society through an industrial society, to now experiencing an information society. In order to process all that information, we need a different mind function.

Now we need to discern the essence of something and it takes a different mindset to discern a relevant piece of information from

5

billions of possibilities of information. Dyslexics have a great ability to sort through huge amounts of information, and intuitively or instinctively pick out the segment that is relevant.

The left brain has a limited perspective, while the right brain has an absolute perspective.

That's what dyslexia has done for me and that's what dyslexia does for anyone who has it. On that basis it explains that whenever humanity has made a major jump in discovery or creativity, there almost always has been a right-brain thinker behind it.

Now we see more and more children with dyslexia, ADD, ADHD and similar labels, because it's an evolutionary process, not a mistake. It's happening subconsciously and under our feet without us noticing. The problem with society is that we haven't accepted that dyslexia is a positive thing, and we still treat it as less or different.

Yes, dyslexics are different, but when we learn how to use and how to harness it better, it will be something that people will look for in children.

Ah, this child is dyslexic, and he or she will go to a special class because these children will produce amazing things in their lifetime. At the moment we still say, "Oh, this child is disadvantaged, we put him in a dumb class." That will change with the sort of work you are doing.

More and more children becoming dyslexic will force us to change our education mechanism. Our failure to not enhance their specialties has filled our jails with these misunderstood individuals.

Eighty percent of inmates in prisons are dyslexic or have ADD because they show the failure of society. The successes are all the brilliant pieces of artwork and the breakthrough in science that we get when we nurture them properly. By failing to realise and harness their potential, will we turn what could be a big win into a big loss.

For me, dyslexia, ADD, ADHD and autism are all related; they are just different by degrees and proportions. A savant, for example, will have an enhancement of a particular brain function; their left brain is able to connect directly with an element in their right brain, which is parallel to their thought process. For example, they are able to recall huge amounts of numbers. Their right or creative brain has the ability to see all those numbers collectively and connect directly to the left brain, which is specialised to order numbers in this instance.

They might not have any ability to communicate emotionally to anyone. They are lost in the world of the right side. They don't see any reason to come out of it. We think they are not here with us. Their attitude is: Why would I? What's the point of me coming out to discuss the breakfast cereal you are having? I am out here, crossing the star patterns of the universe. Are Kellogg's corn flakes more important? Are you kidding?

Autism is much more connected to the right brain and we are trying to tell them that's wrong and to come back to come to the left brain. It's hard to tell someone who is experiencing bliss to ask them to come back and experience the mundane. It's ridiculous. They can, over time, when trained or forced to come out of blissfulness.

My experience of dyslexia is that it is always present, but gradually you teach your brain not to take account of what's happening. The brain is very adaptable and over time it can do that. There is no definite thing which displays one label or another.

Anna, my daughter, is auditory dyslexia, so the words and sounds she hears are not communicated to her understanding in the same way My son and I are visually dyslexic, so what we see is not transposed into an understanding. There are multiple differences of degree of dyslexia. ADD is for me a result of dyslexia.

Dyslexics are seeing a lot more of the universe around them than most other people. They are very easily distracted, as they are seeing one hundred times more information coming in at any one second than other people. Consequently, they find it very hard to focus for any length of time on one thing, as there are so many other things happening. They often run at a faster space, their entire brain mechanism is moving faster, and they are trying to discern so much more information.

When we look at them, all we see is that they can't sit still, they can't concentrate, they seem to be unable to follow one task at a time.

Yes, in a world where we require singular outputs, a child with ADD is uncontrollable, but in actual fact they just do a lot more than we do and they are jamming a lot more into a day. What we are trying to do is slow them down into our left brain pattern, when in fact we should allow them to use their right brain more.

For me, it happened at age seventeen. One day I was walking down the street and what had previously been jumbles of letters suddenly became words—and it happened in a blink of an eye.

I literally blinked and all of a sudden I could see all the street signs in Parramatta Road. All letters suddenly made sense and I could read when I had never been able to read anything before. The dyslexic brain matures at a different rate and when the link between both hemispheres happens, often at a later stage in life, the light goes on. It happened like that for me, but probably not so for everyone.

In order to decipher a word like "cat" with my brain, I have to focus back and ask my left brain to take control. For me, it's a learned mechanism, not a natural order, to put recognition to a word and make the effort to connect meaning and a picture to any word.

One more really important thing: I believe that most people don't see the big picture because they don't have to decipher a huge amount of information. Dyslexics, however, are forced to decipher a huge amount of information in order to operate in the world. What that does is it allows them to see things outside the square. It enables them to be the object, the state of observation and the observer all at once. In order for that to happen you have to have synergy between the two sides of the brain. One day we will all arrive at that synergy ... or we will be born with it.

At the moment, our consciousness is in transition. Some people are beginning to experience that connection: to see the object, which is the left brain; the observer, which is the right brain; and the state of observation.

When you connect both hemispheres, you get a third stage of consciousness that sits up and watches both of them working. That's what enlightenment is: the object, the observer and the state of observation (consciousness that allows you to see both of them).

Dyslexia is the next step on the path of our evolution.

Geoff Englebrecht

Geoff Englebrecht is a successful Dyslexic CEO, aged 61, with deep insight into dyslexia and he also had done a Davis correction program several years ago. I caught up with him and asked him: "What does it mean for you, Geoff, to be dyslexic? What are your thoughts on dyslexia in general?"

MY STORY

Let me tell you the story of my son's transformation from a struggling dyslexic non-reader at the age of eight to an award-winning "young writer" at the age of eighteen.

It is also my own journey from an overprotective, scared mother to becoming a dyslexic facilitator, blessed to work with dyslexic clients of all ages—and all that they have taught me and helped me to become in the past ten years. That journey turned out to be a spiritual quest for myself as much as a discovery of the intricate workings of our mind, for me and for numerous clients.

All stories and examples are true (not claiming that there is only one truth), and all names have been changed to protect people's identities.

Last week I got a phone call from Kylie, telling me about the pain her eight-year-old girl Nellie is going through. With a voice choked in tears, she talked about her daughter's struggles to read and comprehend, her feeling stupid and insecure, losing confidence and, with it, the love of learning. "I don't know what to do anymore. The school has tried to help with a one-on-one tutor one hour a day, but she still doesn't improve," she sobbed. As always, I have to breathe deeply not to get choked up myself, as I understand exactly what she is going through, having been there myself.

I have written this book to help all mothers like Kylie, who call in frustration, feeling the pain of their children. Most dyslexic children or adults sense that there is so much more in them, but they cannot unlock that talent—and it leaves them feeling inferior, misunderstood, isolated, insecure or even depressed.

If you have picked up this book, it is not by accident. You have sensed that there is a potential and inherent gift in what looks like a disadvantage from the outside. This book will reassure you that you are lucky to have a gifted, creative, picture-thinking child ... one who will surprise you and make you very proud one day.

Monday, June 24, 2013

I'm one of twenty proud mothers, sitting at the State Library in Sydney. Most of them are here with their teenage sons or daughters, waiting for the moment when they will receive the book, where their HSC English Extension 2 script, essay, short story or poem is published. I'm here with my husband, as Keanu, the son and author of the theatre script, is on his gap year in Europe, asking us to fill his place. I read and sense the same excitement and feeling of honour and pride in the faces of all these mothers.

There is a middle -aged mum with very thin, grey hair, many anxiety lines in her face, sitting next to me, nervously clutching the invitation. "Has she gone through the same worries about her son that I have?" I wonder.

I cannot help but flash back to when Keanu was in year 3, having lost all the initial excitement of finally starting school like his older brother and sister, who loved the experience and had done so well. He had come to hate school. I remember coming in one day to help the class with reading, as many mothers are encouraged to do, ending up with the "banana group." I don't know who had ever come up with putting these kids into "fruit categories," no doubt to avoid calling them "Advanced," "Average," "Challenged"—"Hopeless"?, but the box of bananas was definitely convinced they were in the "stupid pile."

They were the hyperactive ones, the daydreamers, the class clowns, the bullies, the chatterboxes or whatever creative way they found to distract from the fact that they simply didn't get reading! I was horrified. At the time I was mainly concerned that my son was amongst them—not understanding or knowing any better what was behind the struggle of this lovely group of kids.

Now the Head of the Board of Education is giving his speech, appealing to all the young writers, to keep using their talent, to keep writing until they die.

Wow, if anybody had told me that this could be Keanu, published on page 241, with his play *It's Your Funeral*, I would have thought they were crazy. How a kid can go from the banana group to this select group of fine young writers in nine years, without much help from me, had been beyond my wildest dreams.

Back in Year 3, all I could think was, "Should I have done something when I noticed that he was different to my two older children?" He was about four years of age when my alarm bells first went off. I told him a fairy tale about Hansel and Gretel (which was basically one of THE fairy tales we grew up with, back in Austria), and he listened

13

intently. Obeying some instinct, I asked him to re-tell the story back to me. Well, most of the characters were in his tale, but that's where the similarity ended ... the rest was a beautifully made-up story of his own and, sadly, not the Hansel and Gretel "horror story" I had inflicted on him.

Maybe it just hadn't been the kind of story his mind wanted to deal with at such a young age, I had reasoned, and filed the incident in the "not yet a concern" file in my mind.

"Marcus Keanu Hoi, for his play *It's Your Funeral!*" says Mr. Tom Alegounarias, the president of the Board of Studies, as I walk out to get the award, feeling overwhelmed with joy, gratitude and a sense of astonishment. In Keanu's name I receive the Certificate and *Young Writers Showcase 2012* book.

He had never liked the name we had given him, Marcus, as it was too common in his opinion, and he chose to be called by his second name, Keanu. Always different, always caught up in some kind of drama, I think back with a smile. Out of my four children (I have three sons and the eldest child is a girl; Keanu is the middle son), he was the one who wouldn't sleep through the night, who was noisy, temperamental, active (but not hyperactive)—and accident prone. I belong to an Energy Healing Group and whenever we had a weekend away—without fail—Keanu would be the only child involved in an accident or some bizarre incident. He was the one falling out of bunk beds, was bitten by a cranky old horse and suffered a concussion when he was racing down a forest path with his bike, not knowing how to stop.

14

Come to think of it, this trait of his, to do things without really knowing how to, has stayed with him all these years. He is currently in Austria, working for an IT company for one month, translating their website from German into English ... not being able to speak German! His German skills would be easily matched by anyone who has learnt it at school for one year. When I asked him how he can even consider taking a job without the necessary qualifications—speaking German being a fundamental one—he just laughed and reassured me, "If there is a will, there is a way!" Then there is also Google Translator and he'd be able to "improve on it."

Talking to my friend in Vienna who got him the internship, he seems to be doing a really good job, and they have asked him to come back after his travelling through Europe for two months.

The reason Keanu missed out on being spoken to in German when he was young, like his older siblings, was his inability to speak well, neither in English nor in German, until he was about two years of age. To not confuse him, we rationalised that English would be more important and decided to only speak English from then on. In hindsight, I'd say it was a mistake, as it not only robbed him of learning a second language, the native language of both his parents, but it also stopped his brain from developing these neural pathways so crucial to learn other languages later on, which came so easily to his siblings.

I'm looking through the pages of Keanu's play now, a clever play about a pompous absurdist playwright, Oscar Failfe and his friend and companion, Torval Thogilie, who bounce off wit and insult with one

15

another. That is, until an elderly couple named Barbara and Joseph (his parents' names!), enters the stage, she dressed in a frumpy flowery dress, he in grey overalls, sandals over socks, bland and tasteless?!? Apparently the characters are not based on us. Despite myself I have to laugh when I read on and find out that the character Barbara is termed an oxygen thief and is accused of being the reason why his avant-garde off-off Broadway production of "White Othello" was never shown. "It is your weak mind that couldn't understand the complexities of the cultural perceptions attached to theatre as a form of expression in an expressionless existence … or so it seems. You are the death of theatre. Leave! Leave me now."

Luckily the aim of the play is to question the relevance and value that Theatre of the Absurd provides to an audience.

One of the women who marked all the students' works approaches us to ask if we are Keanu's parents and tell us how much amusement his play had caused them all. She says that he certainly has a possible future in writing.

I can't help but think of Liz, the mother of one of his friends at Beauty Point Primary School, who had also had her input about Keanu's future:

"You must not blame yourself for your son's problems. He may not be good at school, but the world needs labourers, too." That was her well-meaning advice when back then I had confided my challenges regarding Keanu. At the time I really believed they were my challenges, not just his. I am sure she meant to console me—and I have no problem with having a son who is a labourer—but I didn't like the way my son was put into a box, nor the smug look on her face. Even then I had been convinced that my son had the potential to achieve whatever he'd put his mind to. I really believed then, as I believe now, that we all have the ability to change just about anything, if we wish to.

Without doubt you have heard similar "good" advice from your child's teacher, friend, doctor or even a specialist whose services you sought. It might have hit you like a blow to your gut, but I am sure that deep down you also knew that they were wrong.

Most of my clients with children on the autistic spectrum hear it all the time: "Let's face it, there is no cure. The faster you accept this, the better."

There is ample research out now that suggests that our brains are "plastic," meaning malleable; that we can change them when applying different patterns of thinking. Thought leads to feeling differently to acting in accordance with the new way of thinking and creating habits that set us apart from who and how we thought we were. That puts IQ testing into a category of "current state of intelligence" at best, but is mostly useless in the case of our dyslexic learners.

I remember a discussion with Ron Davis (author of *The Gift of Dyslexia*) about the nature of IQ testing. Ron being autistic and dyslexic, having overcome both—or at least the negative aspects of these labels—has given him a unique insight into the nature of this mindset and its ability to be tested in a meaningful way.

He gave us examples of children on the autistic spectrum that wouldn't have shown an IQ over 50, only because they are not "individuated." Once they start to "individuate" (seeing and feeling themselves as being separate individuals, with personalities and egos), the IQ could easily jump to 130, 150 or more. Individuation as well as Concept Mastery and Social Integration, to help the autistic individuals to fully participate in life feature in a book by Abigail Marshall with Ronald D. Davis (*Autism and the Seeds of Change*), a new book about Ron's insights into the nature and possibility to awaken and nurture the seeds inherent in autistic individuals.

Dyslexic children often get labelled as lazy, different and challenged or somehow defective. Nothing could be further from the truth. They are the big-picture thinkers in our world, displaying an inherent ability to view reality from "outside the box," thereby finding creative solutions. And boy, do we need solutions beyond our limited mindset that has placed our species on the brink of destruction. As Einstein so eloquently put it, "We cannot solve our problems with the same thinking we used when we created them."

So why are we as parents so challenged by the perceived lacks, imperfections, troubles of our children? I think for me—and most parents—it comes down to the assumption I formed that I am responsible to do everything in my power to help him, so that he has a chance of "making it in life;" a chance to be happy, become who he wants to be. Without reading skills, how would he get by in life? I think we as parents would feel guilty to just sit back and watch the struggle. Am I right?

In my quest for answers I was really asking for divine guidance, which has always served me well. I didn't want to learn by trial and error; I asked to be shown the right way for my son.

For me, help came in the shape of a book that a friend kindly suggested: *The Gift of Dyslexia* by Ron Davis. Never in my wildest dreams had it occurred to me that he could possibly be dyslexic, nor did I really know what it meant to be dyslexic. Like most people I had only seen a reversal of b/d or p/q for some inexplicable reason as a symptom of a "weird disease."

That book opened my eyes and changed my view—big time! And I found Keanu on almost every page; it was a relief to discover that he was not disabled, that dyslexia is not a disease, but a talent. Keanu's talent is his creative, curious and philosophical way of looking at every aspect of life. In the younger years it showed up as a strength in Drama and Comedy.

The only drawback is that these highly visual individuals find it difficult to reign in the mind from the big picture in order to focus on the tasks at hand. And what a joy to find out that once they get help in the form of tools, visualisations and instructions to creatively solve the fact, that a major part of our language entails non-picture words, they can easily catch up to their peers, or reach their potential, wherever that is set at.

To cut a long story short, it took one week for a dyslexic facilitator to "install the new software" into Keanu's fertile mind and another six months of "homework" to transform all of the two hundred and twenty words that don't have pictures into clay models. In the meantime, I was so inspired by his progress that I trained to become a facilitator myself and have been working in this field for almost ten years now. The training took eighteen months, the last part of it taking place in New Zealand.

While I focused on my own studies, Keanu became more focused on his; he read and re-read all seven *Harry Potter* books, went on to excel in English at high school and chose Advanced and Extension English, as well as Ancient, Modern and Extension History as HSC Subjects. His results astounded us all, especially himself. His HSC (Australian High School Certificate with a maximum of 100) ATAR score of 96.1 was in his opinion topped by receiving a letter from the Board of Studies afterwards, nominating his HSC Extension English essay for a "Young Writer's Award." His Drama Group piece was nominated for "On Stage"—just goes to show that the original quirky class clown is still there.

His confidence, which had always seemed more a drama performance in the past, became a permanent settled state of being.

KEANU'S PERSPECTIVE

Today, July 13, 2013, I received an email from my son, from his gap year in Europe, after I had sent him the part of "his story," asking him to add his own perspective or corrections, if he felt that I had portrayed him wrongly.

Keanu's answers to my questions:

What are your best and worst memories of school?

Worst memories from primary school are hazy because it was a long time ago; however, unsurprisingly I hated being in the bottom reading group for reasons I couldn't explain other than natural order. I have no good memories of English in primary school that I can recall. In high school the first couple of years were not the best for English with the exception of creative writing. My essays got pathetically low marks, my teacher was strict and I was in a strictly talented class. As a competitive person this pushed me to work harder. I have bad memories of being mocked whilst reading Shakespeare, a pet hate of mine when it comes to reading. Positive memories are difficult to pinpoint, I gradually improved throughout high school, fixing up many of my expression problems, and obviously the relative success of my two major works, one creative, the other academic were positive.

What made you go from struggling to read even one page to devouring all seven *Harry Potter* books several times?

21

I read the *Harry Potter* series approximately four to five times in total, my English was improving by the time I finished the first couple of books, I have an addictive personality and *Harry Potter* at the time was the only book I liked and it captured me. The difficulty with this question is that I don't properly remember a period in time where I couldn't read a page of a book; therefore, it's difficult to pinpoint how I progressed. However, if I remember correctly, you read two pages and I read one to start off with, so I knew the story and the plot details, making it easier to read it by myself. Though my English has improved many, many, many fold my reading is still not great, my spelling and grammar average, I still have far to go. The major difference I feel is, that I can express myself clearly and vividly through the written word, whilst before I couldn't whatsoever.

Was the Davis Program that Marianne did with you of help?

Once again it is difficult to say, as it was a long time ago. However, I think it probably did help—possibly to a massive degree, but not sure. All I can say is that I struggle with "trigger words" far less than I used to, but with that said the English language is very tricky and I still feel like I have a loose grip on it sometimes.

Do you still use some or all of the tools you received at the time?

Deep breaths into the nose, out the mouth definitely help before reading; in fact, it helps before almost anything, as it provides clarity and composure. I read best when my mind is balanced and composed, so yes, those tools in memory did and do help.

> Any changes you want me to make on my version of the story of your life?

Ease up on the German bashing; I'm getting a lot better!!

Get rid of the part with "Google Translator;" it undermines the difficulty of the job, as there is far more to it than that.

I'd prefer if you didn't say my ATAR mark, and I didn't receive full marks in Drama, I was nominated for On Stage, for my group piece which implies I got full marks in that one section.

I don't like my school marks being repeated like they're proof of something mothers should aspire the son or daughter to achieve. The education system is moronic, narrow-minded and backwards. It is fixated in a 20th century perspective of academia and how to define intelligence and the HSC is an embodiment of this joke. I can honestly say that I'm ashamed of the Australian education system. I don't think that my achievements can be found in my ATAR, and if Ben gets a low ATAR I wouldn't suggest he has somehow fallen short.

I'm not criticizing you; for all I know you may agree with me, but rather I'm trying to show you why I feel uncomfortable when you repeat my ATAR mark.

BRAIN AND MIND

The title of the book, *The Right Brain for the Right Time* is actually not correct in the way I am going to use the definitions. It should really be called *The Right Mind for the Right Time*. People use the term "right brainers" to categorise anybody who predominantly processes information with the right hemisphere of the brain. They visualise information and get a hunch, feeling or intuition to propel them into action. They are mostly picture thinkers—which I call dyslexics. As visual or kinaesthetic thinkers and learners, their right-brain-approach is really the right approach at the right time—a time where creation is speeding up our perception of reality.

"How does memory get formed and retained? We know a lot about the circuits involved. We know how communication between neurons works but we don't actually know where the memory gets stored," admits Professor Peter Schofield, Executive Director and CEO of Neuroscience Research Australia. *"That's part of the challenge to understand how we lose our memory in dementia."*

Of course this is also part of the challenge with autism, Asperger's, schizophrenia, bipolar disorder and mental health in general. Although dyslexia is not a mental health problem, the answer to the question affects them as much as it affects all of us.

Most scientists try to find memory IN the brain or in the nervous system, which is similar to trying to find the software in a computer. And the files are in the "cloud."

The brain is not the mind. The brain is the translator of Mind, a kind of receiver (or transmitter). The mind is not in our body and it certainly isn't our linear, rational left brain. Neither is it the right side of the brain: creative, visual, intuitive, vast ... Mind is much more than that.

There are many versions and explanations of what the Mind constitutes. I have chosen a simple one that sees the different aspects of our Mind as the:

- Conscious Mind (the tiny 5-10 % of our waking moments when we are truly aware of our creative ability and are living in the moment. The Conscious Mind is switched off at night)

- Subconscious Mind (the vast part of us that never sleeps, remembers everything, files every experience, acts like a default program, has no conscience, no sense of humour, no creative ability, aiming to avoid pain and seek pleasure)

- Super-conscious Mind (also called the Higher Self, the Christ-self, our noble part that is trying to call us to our highest potential, reminding us that love is our true nature).

Beyond the Mind is another field, an even bigger one ... the field of energy and unlimited potential. That is the Quantum field, (also called Morphic, Morphogenetic or Zero-point field), where everything is light and information, present as infinite states of possibilities.

This field of pure energy and light is beaming with intelligence, not yet realised or embodied. In that arena dyslexics can excel, as its language is one of pictures, feelings, emotions. We all have access to it and already use it without realising it. For picture thinkers it's faster— faster to create "heaven" or "hell." They need to be made aware of their power to start to consciously create the experiences they choose to. They and most of us are creating a reality by default, operating on auto-pilot, from a program that was created in the first few years of our lives.

Containing all thoughts, actions, possibilities and sensations, we still manage to draw from this pool of our collective mind the same few experiences that we are programmed to allow. Whatever our imagination can perceive, it's there. From its unlimited potential we consciously and more often unconsciously choose our reality. What we call "reality" could be seen like the software that we download, usually without being aware of it. This software gets received by the brain, in essence all things our personal mind resonates with.

Consider every possibility imaginable exists out there, all the abundance, all the joy, all the love, all the fear, all the compassion— and we choose the same narrow band of "reality." Some people just always meet business partners that rip them off, some always get disappointed, others have a string of "losers" as boyfriends, or seem to have the Midas Touch, turning everything to abundance and success. Are we just randomly dealt the bad cards with every new game of life? Are we at destiny's mercy, born lucky or the tragic victims of life?

If, for example, someone had a childhood with negative experiences or conditioning and they drew the conclusion that they are just not as intelligent, beautiful, powerful, loving or whatever else they may have imagined, or been told, this picture is most likely to be still in their subconscious, running the show. Any experience out there that confirms that false belief and limitation of themselves can be attracted and will serve to confirm their "reality": "See, I told you, it won't work for me. It never has, it never will. People treat me like that because I am not as clever, etc. ..." Naturally this is a simplistic picture, a flippant glance into the whacky world of quantum physics, from my limited perspective, but it will be sufficient to serve our purpose.

We may have children that rely on us to change our filters to enable them to see more of their ability and their potential, which they may not even be aware of. Children, whose abilities are not so obvious, especially in a classroom, are most prone to negative self-talk, and labelling them can lead to a lower level of confidence than they are already experiencing.

However, as much as I don't like putting any label on anyone, I usually find that children are immensely relieved when they find out that they are dyslexic, having thought of themselves as dumb or any other negative label. Especially when I explain that dyslexia is NOT a disability, that it does NOT need to be fixed—and that they are indeed in very good company, with some of the world's largest minds being or having been dyslexic, they are actually delighted.

I tell people that dyslexia is just a different style of learning: it is a visual way of processing the world. That way of learning served Albert Einstein very well.

There is a fine line between labelling children with a disease or a dysfunction, which is often incorrect in the first place, and explaining that dyslexia may seem like a label, too, but in fact is more like a character trait. If someone had the characteristic of being outgoing, fun, gregarious or outrageous, it may also disturb others and that "label" for these extroverts could be seen in similar terms to the dyslexia label. Like the extrovert who can add other aspects to their personality, dyslexics can and should add ways to facilitate their life, especially in the areas of struggle or school work. These new tools are extensions and additions to their lives, not erasing a characteristic. We should not aim to eliminate dyslexia under any circumstances—as much as we would never want to squash creativity or any other characteristic of an individual.

In a 2010 survey amongst 1,500 CEOs of IBM, the number one "leadership competency" of the future was identified to be *creativity*. Right-brain qualities such as inspiration, intuition, creativity, imagination, inventiveness and empathy were named as the currency of the new world. Unfortunately the creativity of school children has continued to decline for the past twenty years, as proven by the Torrance Tests of Creative Thinking. These creative right-brain children are entering the school, but the qualities they are bringing are neither encouraged nor rewarded with good marks.

28

I once read a little-known book by Robert Kiyosaki titled *If You Want to be Rich and Happy, Don't go to School* (Subtitle: Ensuring Lifetime Security for Yourself and Your Children). In it he likened the process of schooling to a reversal of the butterfly cycle. Children enter the school as butterflies and leave the system as caterpillars. He draws the conclusion that our school system is more interested in producing good workers who don't think for themselves and who fit into our economic prototype.

Many people don't realize that there is another way and the way out of the box of a conventional way of thinking, of school and of life in general is through a journey into our minds and souls.

Science will uncover more secrets about the three-pound universe between our ears. Schools will change and adapt to the changing needs of the students—eventually. New ways will be found to harvest the rich and fertile minds of all students, with left- or right-brain dominance. To increase the creativity of the logically minded children is just as important as the help we give the ones who struggle.

In the meantime, however, all we can do is raise awareness, open people's minds and hearts to the true potential and the often hidden jewels of the dyslexic mindset.

It is of importance to pass on tools and strategies on how to apply these creative gifts and this is true not only for our children, but also for each one of us adults. We are the ones holding the field, the space where our children live and thrive.

We need to change our mind, as with it, we will change our reality.

We all know, deep down, that we have signed up for this life with a purpose. We also know that we ought to be and do so much more. We owe it to ourselves, our families and our children to show them by example, and not with words, that there is another way of living, not just surviving. You will be amazed at what you are capable of—and as you change, so will everyone else in your circle.

I intend to write this book from the right side of my brain, as much as possible, to reach your heart. Almost every book on dyslexia that I got hold of has been written from the left-brain perspective. It is filled with research, statistics, data and great advice that will help many parents to cope. There is no reason to write another informative book on the subject—the job has been done, and it has been done well. While the left brain analyses pulls apart and filters through information, the right side synthesises and encompasses, bringing together all parts of self into oneness, not in perfection, but in holistic acceptance.

This insightful and practical book will bring relief and real answers to help mothers to RELAX and shift their focus to empower themselves and naturally create a higher quality of connection in all relationships. Consequently they will hold a safe space for their children to thrive, rather than "fixing" what is not broken in the first place.

WHAT IS DYSLEXIA?

Having worked with hundreds of children in the meantime, I am still in awe of these inspiring and creative minds—and these are the answers to the three main questions that might help you to appreciate the gift and the challenge:

1. What is dyslexia?
2. What are the tools that help?
3. How can we bring out the gift and eliminate the struggle?

I truly believe that our work as parents lies in our own transformation. True and lasting change requires self-realisation—at least it did for me. As for our children, there may be some points that can help to put you at ease and to gain a different perspective. I can highly recommend the book *The Gift of Dyslexia* by Ronald D. Davis to get the fuller picture and reach your own conclusions.

1. *So what does it mean to be dyslexic?*

According to Ron Davis, all dyslexics have three traits in common:

a) They think in pictures
b) They become disoriented
c) They have a low threshold for frustration

Thinking in pictures gives them a great awareness of their environment, an inherent curiosity, intuition and insight. They may also show a multidimensional approach to learning, a vivid imagination, creativity, giftedness shown in geniuses like Albert Einstein, Walt Disney, Leonardo da Vinci, Henry Ford and an endless list of great thinkers, politicians, writers, sportsmen and sportswomen, actors and country or industry leaders such as Richard Branson, Winston Churchill or General George Patton.

Dyslexia is a perceptual talent. Perceiving the written or spoken word in pictures affords much more information. However, the downside of multiple images from multiple angles is the difficulty of reigning that mind in and focusing it onto one thing or one page. Some words fail to conjure up the meaning or picture needed to comprehend what has been read. Most commonly we see reading, spelling, writing, comprehension or math troubles. The same talent has become a liability, especially in schools, where we still educate our young in a mostly auditory manner, not suitable to visual learners.

When picture thinkers cannot make a picture, a part of their brain experiences confusion. Nobody likes that feeling. The mind tries to find an answer, by moving around an object—or the written word—to make sense of it. When looking at an object, viewing it from different sides has often proven useful in the past. However, try to move around a word and all that happens is a different appearance of letters, like b/d/p/q or words (saw/was ...).

The feeling of confusion results in a state of disorientation, caused by a mind searching for meaning. We call disorientation the state of mind, where mental perception does not reflect the reality of the environment. Every one of us experiences disorientation at one time or another, when one of our senses is not in alignment with our body. Let me give you an example:

The other day I drove through a car wash, closed all the windows, and watched from inside my car as the giant bristles moved backwards and forward, washing the sides and roof of my vehicle. Have you ever experienced that sense that your car was in motion just because the outside brushes were? That was my experience and although I knew very well, that my car didn't move an inch, the feeling of disorientation gave the impression of movement. Having the sense of movement or balance out of alignment causes the mind to disorient and record false data.

Daydreaming is a visual, sensory disorientation. The body is present in the classroom or wherever anxiety, panic, confusion or boredom causes the mind to disconnect from it. If a person was forced to read in a state of disorientation, the print on the paper would appear to be blurred or changed in size, shape or appearance. The spaces between words might look like rivers running along the page; the reader might skip lines or words, swap the order of words around, omit or guess words. Additionally, if asked to stand on one leg, they would sway— and that would give away the direction where the mind's eye has moved to.

When I explained to one of my clients that him standing on one leg shows me where his mind is, he told me that he can prove me wrong.

33

Being an excellent sportsman and additionally practising yoga had given him a wonderful sense of balance and he could easily and calmly stay on one leg for a long time. I marvelled at his centeredness and asked if he was able to read a simple text to me while on one leg. Thinking that this would be an easy task, he was amazed how quickly he lost his balance by reading the sentence from a children's book in front of him. It gave him a real-life example of the material that would cause his mind to disorient.

To be in a state of orientation as opposed to the disorientation would mean that the mind has found the right position to perceive reality. It can be likened to somebody wanting to drive a car, where the right position for it would be to sit in the driver's seat. Disorientation then might be a feeling similar to sitting in the backseat of a car, trying unsuccessfully to manoeuvre a car. The proper point of observation, which Davis has come to call an Orientation Point, is a position for the Mind's eye above and behind the person's head. The Mind's eye is our visual point of perception. We see images either from memory or imagined.

In these times of visualisation exercises, when we are asked to imagine a future image of self or a desired outcome, we are actually employing our Mind's eye to bring the images forth. When we read and the images are not naturally revealed, confusion can become overwhelming for picture thinkers, leading to frustration. Confusion and limited comprehension piling up not surprisingly lead to a low threshold for frustration. The level of frustration varies in degree, depending on the "solutions" these children find to cope.

Non-picture words are pronouns, prepositions, some verbs and adverbs, words like "by, for, from, the, so, whether, while ..."—you get the picture—or not.

What if I asked you to think of a submarine? Would that picture come up easily? What if I asked you, to picture a submarine, but not a yellow one, please! My guess is, that you can only picture a yellow one ... **not** is not a picture. I may have an "x" through the yellow submarine, or a crossed-out picture, but in most cases, the colour of the object will be yellow.

Of course, reading Ron's books (*The Gift of Dyslexia* and *The Gift of Learning*) will give you a far deeper insight here. All I can tell you is stories of some of my clients that are typical and will illustrate the three traits:

Lizzy is eight years old. She loves to daydream, to draw, paint and play imaginary games. The teachers get along well with her, as she is not a troublemaker; they just call her easily distracted. Her reading is not bad, the spelling pure guesswork, the writing without punctuation, ideas spreading out without structure. Her math is also basic: she struggles to get the basic ideas of math.

Damien, on the other hand, is always in trouble with the teachers. He disrupts and distracts the other students. Academically he is two years behind his peers. Thinking that his hyperactive behaviour is stopping his learning, the parents give in to the teacher's advice to put Damien on Ritalin. His outlet is his sport, he excels at soccer and his only reason to go to school is recess and the game with friends. Being on a stimulant like Ritalin makes him settle down, but he loses his appetite, sleeps poorly and seems listless. His soccer skills suffer too.

Simon is thirty-seven and, at his own admission, has been able to "bullshit" himself through life. He reads well (omitting a few little words), but when asked after one page what he read, he tells me an entirely different story, with some of the elements of the text, but in such a colourful way, that I am fascinated and almost believe his version. Most people wouldn't truly notice. He also admits that he never understood mathematics, although he is a financial advisor.

Paul is sixty-seven and suffered all his life, always having poorly paid temporary employment, having been on antidepressants all his life. Reading is just hard work, so he only reads the bare minimum necessary. His confidence is low; he never aimed to get help—until now, at the age of sixty-seven, which is admirable.

Lizzy, Damien and Simon are visual learners. They think in pictures and their vivid imagination easily entertains and distracts them. Unfortunately over 70% of the English language consists of non-picture words. Paul finds it hard to visualise. He is a hands-on man, more comfortable with a tactile approach. Like all dyslexic learners they see, hear, feel or sense what they imagine as reality.

2. *What are the tools that help?*

The job of a dyslexic facilitator is to assess the learning style of a client. Using the term dyslexia or arguing that another one might be more appropriate, misses the point here. If you use dyslexia as a broad umbrella term, fitting under it all creative right-brain learners, it best serves the child. A child would sum it up very simply: "If I could learn phonics easily and the auditory approach you have tried to teach me, so far unsuccessfully, I would be able to read by now." In almost any other area of life, we just use a different approach when the original one doesn't bring the desired result. It amazes me that schools don't seem to agree with the logic here, just dishing out more of the same, when the phonic teachings just confuse instead of enable.

Teachers are not to blame here, as this is not part of their training, or only marginally. Most teachers are left-brainers, having enjoyed their schooling—why else would you become a teacher in the first place?

Receiving more and more instructions on phonics (and how confusing is, for example, the different sound of "o", when looking at simple words like: to, too, Tom, ton, tone) doesn't encourage a student to feel success. A sense of dread and feeling stupid replaces the initial curiosity of school and joy of learning.

When Lizzy, Damien and Simon came to me, I was able to give them a stable point of orientation, tools to release tension and anxiety and reduce the stress factor of their energy, which could either be too high or too low. When a person is able to shift the barometer of the energy needed to apply to a certain task, they are much more in control of their own learning. Helping them to become masterful at it is the aim of our work. An optimal orientation point helps them to focus, stay on task and then use these tools while gaining an understanding of the meaning of abstract words.

When the students return home, they can expect to have the confidence, knowledge and ability to learn, but they still have to apply these tools and spend the next months to diligently use them. I always stress the importance to keep these newly formed neural pathways open and deepen them through daily exercises that are given. Research has shown that the brain takes twenty-one days to create a habit. Travelling the neural pathways are therefore of utmost importance after their initial establishment. If parents or children don't take the time and energy during that first month after a programme to apply them with intensity, that opportunity is lost and the success as varied as the focus on the new way of learning. After one month the application can be a simple thirty-minute routine to maintain the momentum and keep the new focus sharp and fine-tuned.

I draw a big mountain for my students, with two hundred and twenty steps, a mountain of trigger words to master in order to climb higher and higher. When they reach the top, they can "fly." With their mother's help (or the wife's, in Simon's case), they have all reached the pinnacle of the mountain and find school and life much less stressful. It always takes time, energy and effort—but it is worthwhile, fun (as all done creatively) and transformational. It is not a lot of extra work, but rather a different way of doing the school work, reading, spelling, writing, etc.

Paul's approach to learning is a different one, not being able to perceive pictures. He may have experienced this ability in his earlier years, and then for some reason or trauma switched it off—or it may never have been a dominant learning style for him. Either way, it doesn't change the fact that the only way for me was to guide him through a tactile approach, in which he achieved the same outcome: orientation.

Having been through enough pain and struggle for six decades, it helped enormously to apply all the tools I am sharing with you later in the book. Paul now loves to read, sees punctuation marks for the first time and was able to share some of the ways of reading without phonics with another work-mate of his. He told me, with tears in his eyes, the euphoria of that man, who had read the entire protocol at some body-corporate meeting, which he had never ever been able to achieve before.

One of the reasons I love my job is the ripple effect it has not only in the life of the clients I work with, but on their families, their life-choices, friends, colleagues and the level of fulfilment.

3. *How can we bring out the gift and eliminate the struggle?*

I am a fan of the Davis Approach, because it acknowledges the gifts inherent in that mindset, always mindful to keep it in place, or increase it. The tools and strategies that we are facilitating are placing the responsibility of eliminating the difficulties into the capable hands of the individuals.

Ron sees the gift of dyslexia as a gift of Mastery:

"Dyslexia is not a complexity. It is a compound of simple factors which can be dealt with step-by-step. At dyslexia's root is a natural ability, a talent. The gift of Dyslexia is the gift of Mastery."
— Ronald D. Davis

A correction programme, as designed by Ron Davis, is a 30-hour intensive, one-on-one experience between a facilitator (and there are many of us to be found worldwide) and a client. It includes tools and exercises to orient the person, which means that they will be able to know for sure if they are focused or not—and with it eliminate the confusion.

The Davis Approach of working with dyslexics is based on the principle that dyslexic strengths and weaknesses share the same root—the dyslexic thinking style. Instead of repetition and drills, which only frustrate these creative beings more without bringing the desired outcome, the Davis work helps dyslexics to focus on the things they can do: think in 3D images and use these gifts to learn differently.

Other tools they are given include an Energy Dial, which the child or adult will be able to adjust to fit the tasks at hand. Together with relaxation tools, ball exercises, a different reading approach (which is not phonics based) and symbol mastery (abstract words are mastered in plasticine) they are well equipped to return to school and apply it in the world at large.

Every dyslexic person has found a different way to use their tools and create their difficulties. Therefore the one-on-one approach best suits a correction. There are often missing pieces in major life concepts that also need attention. Change, consequence, time, sequence, order are just some of the skills that have to be included and mastered.

The Davis Method can address possible math difficulties (having the concept of change, time, sequence and order addressed as being the basic foundation for math), ADD, hyperactivity, hypoactivity, dyspraxia, poor handwriting, auditory sequential processing dysfunction or other associated difficulties—besides the most common corrections of reading, writing and spelling problems.

DYSLEXIA and the PATH to MASTERY

"When someone masters something,

It becomes a part of that person.

It becomes part of the individual's

Thought and creative process.

It adds the quality of its essence to all

Subsequent thought and creativity

Of the individual".

Ronald D. Davis (The Gift of Dyslexia)

DYSLEXIA used as an acronym

D – Discovery (dyslexia and the forming years)
Y – Young Learners
S – School Children
L – Learning at University and Beyond
E – Exercises for Dyslexics (to improve reading, spelling, writing)
X – X-Factor – Different Variations (dyspraxia, hyperlexia, etc)
I – Imagination and the Brain
A – ADD, ADHD

will take the reader through the different stages of dyslexia and offer strategies on how to take advantage of the gifts and talents to not only live up to their true potential but to achieve their dreams faster and with a lot more fun and confidence.

We all have dreams when we are young, until we get told to wake up and "live in the real world," to get a job to pay the bills and support a family. Rarely does someone tell us to follow our heart and make those dreams possible. If they do, they don't tell us how to. Looking around us we realise that about 80% (or more) of us are not living their dream life or reaching their full potential.

However, there are people out there who have achieved their dreams and are very willing to share their secret. Every single piece of advice or strategy on creating a different reality has one aspect in common: the mind has to be able to visualise what we want to see in our life.

That picture of a new life has to be seen, felt and experienced as if it was already here, now. Only then shall we take action, inspired by the new vision, drawing experiences to us that support it.

Guess who are the masters in visualisation?
Guess who feels things that aren't there yet as if they were real?
Guess who could be taught to embrace this gift, train it to be used in the right way—and not by default?

Correct! Picture thinkers are perfectly equipped to play at this. This is the very strength of the dyslexic mind, and of course they are doing it all the time and have always done so. We all do, maybe to a lesser degree, but everybody creates their own reality.

Without the awareness of this inherent power, we don't always create a reality that is desirable. Every time we strongly love or fear something we tend to pull it into our lives like a magnet. As parents we often lack the realisation that the anxiety for our children is the womb for their failure.

If we did, not only would we tell them to relax and take it easy instead of "just concentrate" or "work harder," but we'd apply it in our own lives and lead by example. I am not an advocate of sitting at home and waiting for jobs, money and relationships to keep knocking on our door. I love the idea of inspired action. Yes, we need to take steps to reach our goals, our children need to put in the work to get the grades, but first the mind ought to be crystal clear on which goals are really of essence, helping creation along by being receptive and open to inspiration and guidance. The same applies to our children. They do need clarity on what subjects to choose, on how to attract the right friends, circumstances, people and inspiration into their lives.

How we as mothers or fathers of these gifted right-brained children can best support them at any age and stage of their life is going to be the content of the next chapters.

DYSLEXIA
D – Discovery
Dyslexia and the forming years

"Once upon a time, a girl called Gretel and her brother called Hansel lived with their father and their stepmother in a little hut near the forest. The family was very poor and there was never enough food on the table, even though the father worked very hard all day long as a wood chopper. The stepmother, who did not care much about the children, was resentful about having to share the little food they had with the children and devised a plan to send them into the woods, where they would get lost and never come back home ..."

This is the start of the fairy tale of *Hansel and Gretel* that I had told my son Keanu when he was about three years old. He listened intently, fully fascinated. When he retold the story later, there still was a girl and a boy, but the stepmother had become the witch in the forest and the father was the one who got lost in the woods.

There are ninety-nine words in the beginning of my story above, sixty-nine of them are non-picture words. If you were told a story where sixty-nine out of ninety-nine words were made up in a foreign language, how would you react? The only words that would have been comprehended to a certain degree by a dyslexic child are: girl, Gretel, brother, Hansel, lived, father, worked, stepmother, hut, forest, family, poor, food, table, day, wood, children, little, plan, woods, home. The other sixty-nine words would be either a blank, a guess or a partial comprehension. I think he did remarkably well to come up with a decent story nevertheless.

Although there are many possible indicators in early childhood, none of them are exclusively pointing to dyslexia. In fact, I believe the majority of children at a very early age do have a visual thinking style. Their mind isn't aligned and fully integrated with their body until they refer to themselves in the First Person. People sometimes dismiss the ego as the one part of human nature to overcome or suppress. However, without it, we are not a personality; a separate entity, participating in life. We need the "I" to become that person who is speaking, feeling and thinking. Unless we develop these personalities and individual traits, likes and dislikes, we will most likely be known as "autistic," developmentally delayed, or any other label on the mental health spectrum.

Children who show these dyslexic tendencies are very bright and ideally keep that visual gift, the creative edge. They may develop into "whole-brain" or "bi-hemispheric" individuals, very powerfully mastering both the artistic/creative right side and the linear/logical/sequential left side of the brain.

These dyslexic signals in very young children are just possible clues. They include a difficulty to:

- Pronounce words correctly (Keanu couldn't pronounce the "r" in "run" or similar words)
- Remember names, or recognize names in writing, even their own name

- Put shoes or clothes on the correct way
- Follow instructions, especially lengthy ones
- Comply with instructions, to conform to rules
- Recount a story correctly (as with the *Hansel and Gretel* tale above)
- Sit still while listening (unless watching TV, where visual clues
    are involved)
- Be patient, wait in a queue or their turn (not that this is a
    strength of any young child!)

More often than not, these children learn to walk and talk later than other kids, yet often talk in full sentences when they do.

No child will have all of these tendencies as described above, but if your child scores half of them, there is a possible pattern present.

Most of these points were issues in my son's early development, as well as being accident prone, impulsive, overly dramatic, enthusiastic, fun, creative and many other wonderful traits.

His drawings were never detailed or beautifully executed, but more abstract and unusual, with a great sense of colour and exaggerated forms and angles. Colouring in and remaining within the outline of a sketch is not the strength of a dyslexic learner.

Many children with these characteristics never develop any learning difficulties. However, the talents that are already displayed can be enhanced and the problems can be diminished while these brains are so receptive to change.

There is no need to even focus on a Dyslexia Correction Program. Being so visual and creative, any kind of intervention or attempt to "fix" something will most likely backfire, suggesting to a child that something is wrong. Unless there is a medical problem that needs attention, any other support should come in the form of fun and focusing on positives. The suggestions and playful games I'm talking about will benefit every child, regardless of their learning style, whether they will be dyslexic or non-dyslexic learners by the age they enter school.

Brains need to be stimulated. By giving a child's brain a new experience, its brain will trigger an electromagnetic reaction along its synapses, expand to new areas and grow neurons to create opportunities to work, play and respond differently. Synapses, those connectors between neurons, increase from about 50 billion to 1,000 billion in the first year of a child's life. Imagine the potential.

I believe that a lot of people know this and conclude that their child needs to do more, take part in classes, courses and extension programs. The child gets enrolled in anything from art to zoo excursions. Sport and martial arts for the boys; dance and art for the girls are popular ways to relieve us from feeling guilty that our child might miss out or fail to thrive.

There is a fine line here between stimulating a brain, and stressing the child. Sometimes, doing less—but mindfully—has a far greater effect on the mental, physical and emotional health of an individual than the amount of different activities.

The key is to slow down, to pay attention to the child's needs, their words, body language, interests and challenges. By spending time with our little ones, we need to model in our own energy and behaviour what we want to see happen in their life. I have seen mothers whose mind is clearly on other issues, checking and answering their phones, thinking about tasks that still need to be done, writing shopping lists and multi-tasking while spending time with their child. I have been one of these mothers and know how difficult it is to keep our full attention in the present moment, singularly on the one subject of the moment: our child. Yet, while we are unable to do so, we expect this behaviour from them, especially once they are at school.

Instead of feeling guilty about having to work or not having enough time to spend with our child, remember that it is not just the time spent with them, but the quality of the time. Even if we have to schedule that hour or two into our busy day, it is important to take that "appointment" very seriously and make this time count. It does not really matter if we bake a cake together, go to a playground, swim, laugh, tell stories, play a ball game, a card or board game or have a special outing to the zoo. It all counts. The more fun both parties have, the better the outcome.

When working with young children, I have found the work with their mothers as important, if not more important, than with the small child. Good progress can easily be undone when the patterns that run at home are not changed. These young ones are a direct reflection of their environment. To parents it often seems the other way around: "If only Charlie didn't do that, or Paul behaved differently etc.," their lives would be much easier and then naturally they are seeking to modify the behaviour of a child. This is a task with questionable outcome and motivation.

Most young children I see are displaying hyperactive tendencies. They are the ones that get attention. In my opinion it explains the discrepancy between boys and girls diagnosed with Attention Deficit Disorder (ADD) or Attention Deficit/Hyperactivity Disorder (ADHD). Boys are five to six times more likely to get the ADHD label and the help, which probably stems from the fact that a hyperactive child disrupts a family or classroom far more than a daydreamer. Often boys are more disruptive and vocal than girls. That is not to say that a daydreamer wouldn't need help as much as the hyperactive child. Unfortunately they fall short of that intervention.

The story of Lucas:

Lucas was only four years old when he bounced into my office. He was small for his age, skinny and pale. Bright as a button, full of energy, enthusiasm and curiosity, he started exploring the new environment almost immediately, before he even sat down. His mother constantly reminded him not to touch, not to go into that room, not to climb with his feet onto the lounge. Despite being asked several times to sit down, he ignored her request and continued to jump or climb for another ten or fifteen minutes before he settled down, feet dangling restlessly off the chair. His eyes kept scanning the room. No detail escaped him. He asked, "Why do you have these fuzzy balls? Who is that on the picture? Do you have something to paint?" I could feel the mother's frustration and a feeling of resignation, stress and despair.

"At preschool they suggested to put him on Ritalin or some other drug." She was reluctant, but could understand the teacher's frustration at the same time. Although they told her that he is bright and in some ways ahead of the other children, he wouldn't sit still, disrupted the rest of the children and constantly jumped from one activity to another. He loved the trampoline and ball games, was good on the computer and also at assembling puzzles. He refused to take part in anything that involved a book, writing his name or even touching a pencil.

From the interview with mum I knew that he loved anything to do with dinosaurs and mythical figures; that he liked sweets which mum tried to swap for fruit and healthy snacks, noticing how sugar and coloured cordials made him even more hyperactive.

At that age, I work briefly alone with a child, but then partner with the mother. It is amazing to see how different children behave when mum is not around.

At our first lesson together Lucas was totally focused, engaged and not at all distracted. At no stage did I introduce a book, a pen or anything else that could cause rejection. We used plasticine clay to model dinosaurs, we modelled entire stories that he told me and some letters of the alphabet, especially those that corresponded to the story. We played with balls, taught each other floor exercises and I used these physical games to draw his attention to different parts of the body.

Before going down the road of drugging these children, there are many ways to engage and help them.

There is a window of development in early childhood when teaching phonics makes a lot of sense. A child naturally gains phonological awareness between the age of three and four years. Not all children do, however. Apart from a natural tendency to visualize, there are many possible reasons for this, including multiple ear infections, illness or trauma. Some children may develop dyslexia from our body's inherent ability to compensate for a weakness by developing a strength. In this way any difficulty to hear would create an increased ability in visual perception.

Mothers who talk more to their children help them develop a better vocabulary, as well as a better syntax and context for speaking. It has been said that reading to your child will automatically make them into keen readers, setting a good example and get them into a habit and love of reading themselves later on. This may be very true for non-dyslexic children but I can assure you from my own experience and that of most of the mothers of dyslexic clients I have spoken to, that no matter how much they have read to them, these children were still struggling and very reluctant to pick up a book when at school. It was not until they were given ways to understand what they were reading and finding a book that really captured their imagination that the love of reading set in. This is not to say that reading to a child isn't a fantastic idea in itself.

Ideas to try at home:

- Have rules in your house, but instead of enforcing them in an authoritarian way, explain the "why" to your child. These children (most children) don't respond well to a "because I told you so" order. They will rebel and question your authority. The power struggle will apply your energy in the wrong battle, which you are most likely going to lose.

- Children need some structure and routine to compensate for the chaos they may be experiencing in their daily life, especially when they display high levels of energy. There is no need to be rigid about them. In fact, most children will be able to even help you in setting the boundaries.

- Some of these children may be clumsy or have poor motor skills (gross and fine motor skills). Pushing them into sports (usually their least favourite pastime) may turn them off exercise. Instead, encourage some gentle way to experience their bodies, through Yoga, or some exercises an OT (occupational therapist) can encourage. Once they are more aligned to their bodies they get better with ball games and will enjoy some kind of sport. By the time I see a child with dyspraxia, they are usually already at school and struggling to read, which is a very common by-product of the disorientation they experience.

- Reinforce their creative gifts. Make up stories, create puppet shows, draw, paint, make sculptures, play memory games, age-appropriate board games, charades, treasure hunts—your imagination is the limit.

- Draw three different patterns on a sheet of paper for them: a dot, a straight line and a wavy line. Tell them the difference and then draw these same shapes with your finger or a closed pen gently on their back, left or right arm, on each thigh, the back of their hand etc. They shouldn't see it; just feel the symbol on their body. Tell them to close their eyes, or look away and make it a game. It may surprise you, but there are some parts of the body that they may not feel any differentiation of shape. Some children may know it only on one leg or arm, not the other. Simply by playfully experiencing these tactile sensations, you have opened new areas of the brain that correspond to the different body parts.

- Only after the three shapes can be clearly felt and named, should you move on to simple letters and repeat the exercise. Only then does it makes sense to write letters on different sensory materials, into the sand, follow the wooden shape of a letter, or the fuzzy velvet touch or in water, etc.

- Create a stimulating environment for the child without overstimulating the senses. The more input they have in the creation of their rooms and activities, the more you can be certain that it doesn't overwhelm them.

- Draw five circles on a piece of paper and colour them differently. Ask them to take a look, make a photo with their mind, and then recall them in the right order, from left to right, then from right to left. A visual learner will be far more easily able to do that. Depending on their age, there may be more or less coloured circles.

Whatever you do, have fun with it and be light-hearted. Learning to read is not a race and those who start later are in no way disadvantaged in the long run.

DYSLEXIA
Y – YOUNG LEARNERS

"The school has called me in again talking of disciplinary actions and possibly expelling my son," Jane explains on the phone, talking about the struggles of her son Tony. "He is the loveliest kid at home—and apparently turns into a monster at school. He refuses to pick up a pen, look at a book or follow their instructions." I almost drop the receiver of the phone when she goes on to tell me that her son is only five years old and at kindergarten. "Oh, yes," she confirms, "They are writing short essays already. It's quite a proud and competitive school with an excellent reputation."

When I meet Tony one week later, he appears as the most gorgeous young boy with big brown eyes, very alert and well behaved. I assure him that this is not going to be a test or anything like school and all I want is to have a chat with him and his mum. I am intrigued at how early some schools are gearing their young charges towards academic achievements, at the expense of the arts, crafts and sport that used to be a major part of the kindergarten experience.

Even more does it amaze me to hear about the disciplinary consequences of his apparent lack of cooperation at school. After refusing to leave the classroom to sit in the library as a punishment for not "obeying their orders," the teacher tried to physically remove him, while Tony hung on to the door frame and tried to bite the teacher's hand. According to the mother, who was called in by the school to discuss the future of her "dangerous" child, the teacher is apparently so scared of him and his violence that she refuses to keep Tony in her class.

I ask Jane if the school did any kind of testing or psychological assessment to discern if he has learning disabilities or what I would call dyslexia. Jane assures me that they have never felt a need to test him, despite her insistence (having had an older son who had learning difficulties that had plagued him during his entire school experience). The school is convinced that he would be fine if only he'd take up the tasks that are put in front of him. In any case, how can they assess academic performance if he refuses to comply?

Like my son, Tony had also been looking forward to going to school, eager to be a "big boy," to learn and have fun with his friends. For both of them—and I am sure many other children like them—the reality was quite different. It can range from a dislike to terror. If my son had shown the same amount of resistance to conformity he would have received attention at an earlier age, too. Fortunately, it's never too late to help these children, and the only advantage Tony will have over my son Keanu is a shortened period of discomfort.

Symptoms of children at kindergarten and the early years at school include difficulties to:

- Learn to read "simple" words or keep up with the class average in reading and spelling

- Write the letters of a word in the same or similar size and shape

- Put all the letters in the proper position (often reversing b, d, p, q, 9, 6, etc.)

- Stay focused on one task, especially if the task is related to school work

- Perform under pressure like a timed spelling test

- Understand "time," tell the time or estimate how much time was taken up by a task

- Experience a good sense of direction

A lot of children lack appetite due to feeling anxious and end up bringing their lunch home again—or leave it in the bin. They might also appear pale, spacey or moody.

Despite their best efforts, every task takes them much longer to perform than other kids, which naturally leads them to feeling frustrated and increasingly insecure. Often they end up dreading school and searching for ways to avoid the experience by any means possible: sickness; being physically present at school, but not mentally; disrupting the class through humour or misbehaviour; sometimes lying to cover up their weaknesses or finding very creative ways to cope.

Words in themselves are nothing but meaningless symbols for a person who has been able to make sense of his world in images and often reached a far more detailed explanation of their reality. Thousands of tiny details that usually escape the attention of us adults and other children are registered in their minds. Curious, sensitive and intuitive by nature, they have installed huge amounts of data in their brains, not always accurately perceived—but always associated to a picture or feeling.

Filled with curiosity, they can't wait to get to school. The first symbols and words are soon added to their learning environment. Symbols devoid of meaning. Symbols and letters that confuse. While trying to switch and turn them any way possible by racing an inquisitive mind around them, they still don't find a clue or reason for their existence.

Reversing letters has its root in the ability of these children to get a view of them from different angles. When closing your eyes, can you picture the letter "n" as a 3D shape? Can you also imagine that your Mind's eye wanders all around the object, having the straight line on the right side, or seeing it as a "u"? You can try that with "b" and make it into a "d" very easily. Right? Together with turning the letters upside down, their whole world has been equally flipped. What appeared fun and easy, is now confusing and nauseating.

While the majority of the class has finished a project, the dyslexic child is still trying to make sense of the first letter or word. What has been an enormous process of picturing many variations and angles of a letter, a process of trial and error, looked like a failure to pay attention or focus on their task to the teacher. Slightly irritated, or very kindly reminding the child to get on with the work, to not guess or to finally catch up can cause a huge emotional reaction and with it the loss of self-esteem.

Like in the case of Tony, many children stop trying after that initial difficulty which they often perceive as a big failure. They are upset and have different ways of showing it. We all have learned a variety of emotional responses that have worked in the past to give us relief. Tony rebels. He knows he is not stupid, but believes that everybody else has formed that opinion of him. His teacher doesn't express it, but the message comes across nevertheless. The more she tries to discipline him or show her authority, the worse his reaction. There often is a point of "what's the use, I'm just no good, I might as well not even try."

Dyslexia and Reading

When reading, the early books with pictures that add to the comprehension of the text will cause less trouble than chapter books later on. Guessing the words from reading the first letter, in connection with an image, often comes in handy. Being highly intelligent, these children sometimes remember the entire text and, rather than reading it, recite it from memory.

Reading in schools is almost always taught phonetically. It does help most children—children who are auditory learners. Linguists believe that the language should be analysed and taught in phonemic terms. Phonemes are the basic units of a sound, the abstractions of a set of speech sounds. Although the English alphabet only has five vowels (a, e, i, o, u), it has thirteen to twenty-one vowel phonemes. There are three major issues with phonemic awareness for dyslexic learners:

1. Sounding out doesn't come naturally to a picture thinker and is a very difficult task to master.
2. Grouping phonemes together to speech sounds and words implies linear or sequential awareness, which again is a left-brain ability, and is not strongly present for visual learners.
3. Phonemes are considered the sound translation of the alphabet, which are the written symbols of the phonemic sound. Spelling and pronunciation of a word can be very different and highly distorted by different dialects and foreign origin words. This inconsistency creates great confusion to the dyslexic individual already struggling to come to terms with the meaning of the word.

Many children that have come to me with different dyslexic variations have reported feeling nauseous when having to sound out a word. Others find it hard to overcome the habit of the drill they have been objected to and keep on struggling to find the appropriate sound to come up with the correct answer.

The young learners are at an advantage here, if they correct dyslexia at this stage and don't have to "un-learn" strategies and avoid going down the track of trying to compete with the auditory learners on the subject of sounding out. They need to be taught to utilise their strengths and talents to learn the same material as the auditory student, yet coming at it from another angle.

It reminds me of Albert Einstein's quote on our Education System:

"Everybody is a genius. But if you judge a fish by its ability to climb a tree it will live its whole life believing that it is stupid."

Einstein knew what it meant to feel stupid at school, having struggled at school himself due to his own dyslexia.

Ron Davis has come to the same conclusion and devised a way to facilitate the process of reading, spelling and writing for the visual and tactile learners.

Before starting the reading process, the elements of a word, each single letter, needs to be crafted in 3D. With the use of plasticine, the upper and lower case alphabet has to be created by the student, regardless of their age. It always amazes me just how many letters that appear to be known show up as confusing triggers. I have helped a few of my clients who had done the alphabet with their mums already, following the instructions in Ron's book *The Gift of Dyslexia*. It is difficult to pinpoint just where confusion is and how to tell the difference between the clear understanding of a letter and other aspects that have attached themselves to the meaning of some of these letter of the alphabet. Contacting any trained facilitator might help to establish a solid basis for the future of reading and learning by eliminating any possible misunderstanding of symbols.

Symbols also include punctuation marks, which at this early age will be limited to full stops, question marks and some of the comma uses. There is no point in starting to read if there is a possibility that symbols are confused and not fully understood—or the assembly of letters to words don't make sense and the appropriate meaning in the mind of the young child.

You may be amazed how few children really know the alphabet … yes, most of them know the alphabet song, but that doesn't guarantee that the letters are known. For example, I have seen a few children who believed that l-m-n-o-p is one sound, simply because that's how it sounds in the song.

We also need to be aware of the state the child is in when we start with any kind of intervention. A facilitator is well trained to help a child to establish the perfect state of orientation, depending on their learning style, age, ability and present moment awareness. However, some parents are very capable in helping their own child, simply using Ron's book *(The Gift of Dyslexia)* and its instructions. I wasn't one of them.

Even after I had done the training to become a Dyslexia Facilitator, I chose to get another facilitator to work with Keanu, as I found that I am too close to my own child to truly make a change happen.

Apart from the problems many young learners display, problems that mainly show up at school, there will be the same intelligent, curious and fun child at home—often only hampered by anxiety around their performance at school. Naturally they will display some frustration at home, usually with their own siblings. On the other hand they may be experts in building Lego structures, drawing amazing artworks, finishing puzzles in record time or showing other great abilities.

As much as parents know and appreciate the intelligence in their children despite the struggles, assuring them how clever and wonderful they are doesn't seem to be enough. Only when a child realises its own potential and proves its abilities to apply that intelligence in the classroom will they develop the self-confidence needed to correct their learning problems.

Ideas to try at home:

- Don't introduce paper and pencil to a young child that might be struggling to read—as they need to get a three-dimensional view of the letters first. Get them to make these letters in clay or plasticine, copying the image of a letter you show them. The letters don't need to be perfect, but accurate. There is no "perfect" size but they should be approximately the thickness of a pencil and the more or less the size of a chicken egg for capital letters, smaller for the lower case alphabet.

- Introduce one letter at a time; get them to make it in capital and lower case, then going on a search for them—in the street on traffic signs, in parking lots, headlines in newspapers, etc. Get them to re-create it in sand when on the beach, made out of small pebbles, drawn with chalk, on spilt sugar, on the steamed up windows or any other creative way you can think of.

- Find words starting with the letter he knows, without going too much into the spelling of it.

- Write the letters on their back and they will guess it, or on other body parts. The more fun you have, the better.

- Always ask the child to take a deep breath and feel the feet on the floor and make sure they are present when you work or play with them. Awareness of your own energy and to be in your own body is of utmost importance. The mother holds the space and the child will follow.

- Eventually all the alphabet is mastered and fully understood. It takes as long as it takes. Having full mastery creates a firm foundation for later and worth every minute and hour spent on it. There are twenty-six letters to master and it could be done in twenty-six days.

- Most children don't know the alphabet, only the alphabet song. Get them to take a mental picture of their own alphabet and see if they can recall the letters in the right sequence. Can they do three letters in a row, five letters or more? Can they recall them in backwards order?

- If the child has a hyperactive tendency and you may think that they will learn best when they sit still, you may try the opposite: Get them to see and recite the alphabet while jumping on the trampoline or catching a ball.

- A ball game with small koosh balls (stringy rubber balls the size of tennis balls) are great to throw to a child while they are standing about one meter in front of you, later further away. If they can, ask them to stand on one leg and get them to catch the ball. First they might catch it with both hands, then eventually with one hand, and later you move to two balls and ask them to catch one in each hand. There are many variations to these games and they can be a lot of fun. The better a child gets in balancing on one leg, the better their ability to focus.

- Just do what is fun and watch for changes. Notice what is different, not what is the same. Whatever you pay attention to you will see more of. If you want to see more focus, pay attention to any signs of it when they do their clay work or guessing games.

- Don't ask a child to concentrate, and instead ask them to take a deep breath and relax before putting their attention to a new task, any task.

- Have many small breaks, especially if the focus wonders, change to another activity. Usually a physical, creative or sporting break balances a child better than watching TV. If a child just wants to work on and do more and more letters, it might be a sign of a habit to rush through and get it over and done with. In that case, just introduce a couple of letters and avoid the temptation to get into the groove of an old practice.

- Any activity is designed to change or create new neural pathways. In order to see something new, it needs to be consciously introduced and integrated.

- Memory games with pictures are a good way to sharpen the skills these children already have.

- Tell them the beginning of a story and ask them to make a movie in their head and continue the storyline—so the film becomes a co-creation. If they like the story, they can draw it or make it in clay. You can even write it to their dictation and together with their drawings make a children's book out of it.

- Your imagination is the limit. Have fun and enjoy the bond that it will form between you and your child.

DYSLEXIA
S – SCHOOL CHILDREN

Keanu was in Year 3 when I was roped in as a mother helping to read with the class. They gave me the "banana group," apparently the bottom of the "fruit chain." Keanu was in it, and so were five other boys and no girls. Tom was the naughty, noisy one who disrupted everyone and had a short attention span; Jack tried really hard, was clearly flustered and guessing most words, using any visual clue from the picture above; Finn was the class clown and found humour a good way to distract from the fact that he read poorly and didn't understand what he read; Paul appeared bored to tears; and Ryan just wasn't present, daydreaming or commenting on the fly that had just landed on the window sill. Keanu was the dramatic class clown, yet tried hard to decipher the words to please his mum.

At the time, I had no idea what was wrong with any of them, had not heard more about dyslexia than the myth of the b and d reversal, which I assumed was a brain-malfunction. I can relate to people's lack of compassion or understanding, as I was no different. As much as it frustrates me today, when teachers tell me that "mothers seem to believe their children are geniuses, not wanting to face the fact of the opposite"—I was no different. I am far less judgmental today toward any behaviour a child may display and appreciate the compassion gained from more knowledge about the label "dyslexia."

When someone tells me nowadays that there is this horrible bully in their child's class and what action the school ought to take against him I have a totally atypical reaction to it to most people. My first thought goes out to that bully and I wonder what is really going on in his mind, where his deeper issues lie and why he displays the undesirable behaviour. My heart also goes out to the child who gets bullied, asking the same question. Which type of child is usually the subject of bullies?

I believe we don't spend enough time empowering our children or teaching them in which way to behave when faced with a bully. More importantly, we should teach them what type of energy we need to be in to not even attract a bully.

Some of the symptoms you may find in dyslexic school-aged children are a difficulty

- To read, write and spell at the class or age level

- To comprehend what was read

- To read out loud in class (it can be a horrific torture for some children)

- To pronounce words correctly (especially complicated terms) and often using choosing simple words to avoid the embarrassment.

- To recognize rhyming words (do the words life and loaf rhyme?)

- To articulate themselves. Often the phonological chaos in their brain makes them avoid unfamiliar words or switch letters around, e.g., animal might become 'aminal'

- To put their wonderful ideas into words, in a spoken or written form, sometimes both

- To develop a good sense of time (often it's hard to guess how much time has passed or how much time a task will take). Being late can be a part of the missing concept of time.

- To follow sequences or understand the order of sequence, how things follow one another in a linear line. The concept of sequence is a left-brain strength, but also one of the pillars of math.

- To create or maintain order. While a child who is even more on the right-brain spectrum or ASD (autistic) often needs order and can become obsessive compulsive in their need to have things constantly at the same place or time, dyslexic children rarely display these OCD traits.

- To keep their attention on one activity for the length of time it is required. Mainly children who are diagnosed ADD or ADHD have trouble in this department.

Naturally not all these characteristics are present in every student. Some of these creative beings have also added their own special blend of symptoms, often combined with their own set of solutions.

Often these solutions are also crutches provided by well-meaning teachers or parents trying to facilitate their lives. They are usually ways to help them memorize the spelling of words and similar to the alphabet song. As much as the alphabet isn't really mastered by singing it, spelling remains an equal issue. Being able to spell a word doesn't add meaning to it—and the lack of meaning is usually the main reason for a failure to comprehend a text. Words without pictures are words without meaning for most dyslexic children.

Sometimes parents tell me that their child reads well, but when listening to them, I have noticed that they leave out or change the "little" words. Prepositions, pronouns and other "small" words often lack meaning and are seen as boring fillers. Older children may have acquired the knowledge of these words, but upon closer inspection, the meaning is usually limited or different to the dictionary. It is wonderful to see the certainty that mastering these words can provide. Then the confidence in any area of learning improves.

Most of the clients I see are between eight and thirteen years old. The transition between primary school and high school brings the realisation that from now on it is not about learning to read any more—but about reading to learn. Any hope that primary school will live up to the promise that "they will get it" has evaporated. Fear of the big school is leading to anxiety and other emotional triggers, who

72

are not only the result of their learning disabilities, but often end up causing them additional barricades to studying patterns.

Dyslexia is not difficult to correct, yet tens of thousands of children who are struggling at school and could be helped, are remaining undiagnosed. If they get help, it is often in a way of tutoring—although they will benefit from the one-on-one attention, they are still getting instructions the same way as auditory learners. Getting a phonetic education with more intensity does help a small percentage of children, especially those who find it hard to focus in class. They may get distracted and zoom out, thereby missing a big chunk of their education. However, children on the dyslexic spectrum will not improve significantly, regardless how often they hear the instruction. They most likely end up feeling inferior and stupid. "Despite all this effort on the part of my tutors, I still don't improve," said Danny and anyone could read between the lines how he felt about himself.

The number one reason children are coming to me is literacy or the lack of reading ability or comprehension. Parents are at the end of the road, spending hours every afternoon or into the night, helping their children doing the homework. If a child is of moderate to high intelligence, has great work ethics and doesn't achieve at class level despite all the hard work, dyslexia will be the main cause for it. If, additionally, there is a family history or a parent or grandparent who struggled at school, diagnosed or undiagnosed, the probability is higher still. Recent studies have confirmed that dyslexia runs in families, yet is not entirely genetic. Even with a genetic predisposal it takes an environmental trigger or a curiosity to perceive more of the world to develop dyslexic qualities. Not every dyslexic person I've seen had a dyslexic family member, but the majority of them have.

Often the profession of the mother or father indicates the underlying creative vein and the talent in place. Not all parents make the connection but they often see the parallels between their own experience and that of their child. As a result they can feel their pain and understand their suffering.

The ideal scenario would be a school that caters to the creative souls and nourishes their talent at the same time as it helps them to creatively solve their learning difficulties. School should be fun and stimulate a child's unique strengths. It should awaken the seeds of what they already know, open the minds to new areas of interest. Unfortunately I don't know of such a school in Australia, but would be very interested and happy to stand corrected. I have heard of some charter schools in the United States of America that have achieved some great results in that area. I know of a few schools in New Zealand where the Davis strategies are getting implemented in class or additionally in a special classroom that is seen as "the cool school" every child in the school wants to be a part of, not the dreaded "special-ED" classes that add more stigma and separation than solution. I have seen severely traumatised children out of these "special-e" groups, children that have continued on their downward spiral that was aggravated by the cocktail of various mental, social, psychological or physical disabilities in these groups.

The second best solution would be a correction program facilitated by a trained practitioner, where in a one-week program the learning practices and lives of the right-brain individuals get completely turned around, their confidence skyrockets and they take responsibility for their own literacy and future learning. There are many Davis dyslexic facilitators worldwide, but there are also equally wonderful therapists out there, making a big difference in their clients' lives. I believe that any therapy that can add confidence and new tools to use their gifts to visualise or to create is of utmost importance.

Some parents don't feel that they can afford to spend their money on extra expenses in their child's education. How can we afford not to? What is the price we ultimately pay when we fail to address the issue altogether?

I have known mothers who truly cannot afford a program and have been committed to spend the time and energy on helping their son or daughter. They have read the book by Ron Davis, *The Gift of Dyslexia*, and applied his methods themselves. I truly admire them, as I know how much hard work they have put in. For them and for everyone who likes some strategies, I have added some helpful tips:

Ideas to try at home:

- As with the preschool group, always start at the most basic instruction. Don't expect anything or make assumptions. The alphabet is the basic unit of a word—and there are always some letters present that are either not clear or have certain triggers attached. Have your child make the alphabet in clay:

upper case and lower case. Make sure they slow down to say all the letters individually and know what they look like, what they sound like, which words start with these letters, etc.

- Make sure the child is fully alert and present with you when you work together. It is much better to work in short spurts of only one hour with a break every fifteen minutes or less. Whenever you perceive that the child gets distracted or tired, call a break or interrupt for some activity to get the blood flowing and oxygen into their brain. Start again with a deep breath and great focus.

- Never force a child. Look for a point of motivation. Ask them what they would like to achieve, or what they would like help with. I once worked with a teenager who was overweight and hypoactive and hard to motivate. It wasn't until we found the one area where he really wanted change that we could make progress with his input: He wanted to have a friend. After some discussion he concluded that he would possibly be able to make a friend if he was more sporty, as most boys his age where playing footy or basketball. But being overweight was not helpful. I asked if he was willing to accept my help. After more discussion he agreed that a bit of exercise, like riding his bike, which he used to enjoy when he was younger, could be of benefit. It just has to start somewhere. The bike riding turned out to be fun for him and his mum too and lead to him joining his brother at the gym, lifting weights. As his body slowly changed, his confidence and his willingness to address other issues around learning developed too. The original motivation met and his goal of having friends achieved for the first time in ages led to a new ease that he had never known. Often the initial step is difficult to make, and even more difficult to maintain and turn into a habit. But once this is done, the road seems to be established and subsequently easier to travel.

- Don't overload the agenda with a multitude of changes all at once. Always start with a small change, one that seems to be the most important one for the child—but persevere.

- Listen to the child read out loud for a short time and notice if there are words missing, changed, mispronounced or confused. Don't correct him, but ask him to spell the word—not sounding it out, but spelling it like the alphabet would have been spelt. Wait a short while and tell them the word without making a big deal of it. Often the easiest words are the hardest for a dyslexic child. They sometimes have a conceptual meaning, a distorted one or none at all. These words are the ones the child should learn to master and get help with. (Refer to *The Gift of Dyslexia* by Ron Davis). Sentences with a long row of these words can be most unsettling and you'll notice deep confusion setting in. Example: *He saw that the one who had held him up was the same that had been there before.* (A sentence like that shows a long row of abstract words and would cause a reaction that could be

77

interesting to observe. Some children might even feel nauseous, dizzy or simply not comprehend anything they read nor any future text. One confusion often leads to a compounded reaction, if reading on without a break.)

- Is your child reading without stopping at full stops, question marks or exclamation marks? Point out the importance of punctuation marks. They are the Stop Signs indicated by the author and serve to create a picture before proceeding to read on. Without stopping the meaning becomes tangled up. Example: *Now the man clearly needed help. From the left side a small child approached.* (Without stopping it would mean that help was needed from the left side. Yet that wasn't the intent of the author.)

- If your child is struggling at school and falling behind, some teachers might suggest repeating the year. I have found that this practice does not benefit a dyslexic child. Repeating a year will reinforce what they already believe—that they are not clever enough ... and that is simply not true. The way that things are taught won't change by reliving another year of agony. The failure to learn to read is usually a failure to teach these children in a way they can understand.

- These children often display a low threshold for frustration and don't take criticism well. Working with your own child is often even harder than somebody else's child. If you are trying your luck at this, here are some points that might help:

- Don't make your requests sound like orders.

- Ask questions rather than telling the child what they have to do. ("What do you think would help you to remember this?", or "How can you make a picture of this in your mind?", or "What do you see or feel when you read this word or phrase?").

- When they read a passage, ask specific questions about the meaning, not a general "What did you just read?" Instead find out how the main character would have felt in that situation or who the author would have referred to with "it" or how many people were in that room, etc.

- Be light-hearted and fun

- Invent creative games to make the task more interesting

- Find board games or card games that they are good at, where there memory gets improved or their creativity can shine. It will improve their confidence and with it their performance.

- Don't rush them. It is important to sometimes slow them down if they have a tendency to rush through things.

• Sport is an important way to add balance in body and mind. Ball games help the coordination and any team sport increases their spatial awareness. Many dyslexic children excel at sport. It can be a way to channel excess energy and reduce frustration. The ball games described earlier, catching two "Koosh" balls while standing on one leg are an excellent way to sharpen the focus, harmonise the two hemispheres of the brain (especially when having to cross the mid-line while catching the balls on either side) and increase coordination. Additionally, the increased focus can be used to learn the alphabet, to count or multiply or get a good right-left coordination. An instruction that the balls will only come to the left side (or the right side) will enforce the sense of direction and eliminate any right-left confusion.

- Reduce the time spent in front of TV or playing computer games or PlayStation. Instead of being regimental about it, encourage family activities, camping trips or family games.

DYSLEXIA
L – LEARNING at UNIVERSITY and BEYOND

These are the questions I have asked of students, facilitators and adults with dyslexia—to gain insight into their perspective of their own strengths, weaknesses and generally the perception of dyslexia.

Dylan, Uni student, 21

"Dylan, how do you find University, since finishing your program recently?"

I was not diagnosed with dyslexia until before my 3rd year of university at the age of 20. Before then I was frustrated and hard on myself for not getting the grades I thought I deserved. I just thought I was either lazy or maybe not as smart as I thought I was, thus destroying my confidence and motivation. I always thought there was something not right; like I had A.D.D or some other issue, but never dyslexia because I could read and write to some level.

After the diagnosis and treatment everything made sense. It made sense why my H.S.C score was so low. It made sense why even though I knew all the answers in class I could never put it on paper in tests. It made sense why I was the only kid in preschool who could not spell his name. Dyslexia does not define me; however it is still a part of who I am.

Also after the treatment I gained a confidence in my work that I could not imagine ever having, because I now know how to work with my Dyslexia.

81

University is going great and I have figured out ways to work to my strengths. The Uni isn't as helpful as I expected; however, I have adapted to what they expect and I am finally succeeding at Uni.

At University I am currently studying advertising and that means I have a lot of group tasks. Unfortunately I still struggle with the reports but in groups I have discovered that I am a vital member, a great leader, a great presenter, an excellent creative problem solver and recently I quickly taught myself Photoshop and could create fantastic visuals that could get our group mark from a credit to a high distinction. I am constantly improving on these skills. Also with these skills I see myself being very successful in the advertising industry.

I am extremely grateful to you, Barbara as I cannot see myself being this successful this early without the treatment.

Lynne has worked with a former "Wallaby"-Rugby player and an English Rugby Union Player.

They were both in their thirties when they came to her, having hardly any reading skills, wanting to create a new life for themselves. "Lynne, what was their motivation to wanting to learn to read at the age of thirty-five? What was it like to work with them and could they read after having done a Davis program to correct dyslexia?"

Both of these clients I worked with realised in their mid-thirties that life as they knew it was over—and how they had functioned prior to seeing me was with old solutions. When they were at school they both couldn't read, they had a lot of trouble academically, but they

82

were clever, had good people skills and were able to talk themselves out of being in school. They were good at Rugby and made that the main focus point, simply to avoid school and reading. They made sure they were on the team— on the top team, all the way through primary and high school.

At school, they were bullies, avoiding schoolwork. They didn't want people to know that they couldn't read, or to make the assumption that they were dumb, so being a bully was a good cover. They both told me that they were in the Rugby team to avoid school, not because they love the game. The game was easy for them; they didn't have to work hard at it and used it to escape. Both of them got a career, one playing for the British Team in Rugby Union, the other for the Australian Wallaby Team. The British guy got to the top by bullying people, the captains, his coaches, managers—everyone was scared of him and they walked on eggshells around him.

After he got too old and finished playing for England, he got married and realised that his life was redundant. He didn't have a role; he didn't have a purpose, as Rugby had been his life. He had been recognised everywhere and found he could bully his way through life. The Wallaby player had a very similar upbringing, career and also marriage. They both married successful, capable women; both wives were in marketing, one running her own company, one employed by a big multinational marketing firm. That was their security.

Both realised in their mid-thirties that whatever they wanted to do past their career would involve some reading skills. The English player wanted to do the program because he wanted to read a book to his child. In tears, he told of his desire and for the first time he was lost and didn't have a strategy in place, as he couldn't bully his way into his reading ability. He had moved from England to Australia to make his transition to a "normal" life. The Wallaby player was living in Sydney too at the time and both realised that they didn't have any skills outside Rugby that could get them a job.

Both of them were so similar. They didn't like their roles in the Rugby team. They hated having to talk to the media after every big game, when they were interviewed. They used to dread that moment, the cameras coming up to them, reporters asking them questions about how they felt about the game. In their mind they already had the idea that they were perceived as bullies or not too bright. In their state of anxiety they often stuffed up and hated the interviews. Although playing for England and Australia, they were not happy in their roles. It was amazing. So the reason for doing the program was to change their life and their career.

By the end of the week, they were reading, in tears. Both of them said that if they had known about this when they were young, their whole lives would have been entirely different.

During the whole week there were many tears and it was a big deal. The two programs were of course done separately, many months apart, but it struck me how similar their stories were.

Report from a facilitator who was working with a teenager. "How was it, working with a shy, struggling teenager who couldn't read?"

I worked with a fifteen-year-old boy who came to me to do the week-long program. The day he came in for the assessment, his body was concaved, his hands protecting his heart, his head was down, his face was full of red acne, and he couldn't look into my eyes. After the consultation, he was making eye contact, because for the first time, he told his mum, it all made sense to him. I could tell from his body language that he knew exactly what I was talking about.

When this boy walked in on Monday, he simply couldn't read a word. He stumbled over every single word. He was excited, but he still didn't make eye contact. By lunchtime, he was looking at me; he had read his first sentence, ever.

By the end of the first day, he was standing up straight, he looked at me in the eye, his energy was high—and he already looked like a different person.

His mum called me that evening and thanked me. After the first day she had the boy back that she had lost when he started school.

By Friday, after he had been with me for the whole week the kid came in, standing tall, his acne completely cleared up, he was reading and he looked so different from the person who walked in just a week ago.

It wasn't just a different personality, it was a different boy. It was phenomenal. We always have big changes, but this case was huge. And this was a fifteen-year-old high school student.

This mother rang me, in tears. Her son was in his room, reading *The Lord of the Rings*. I cautioned them to take it easy with the reading, especially in the beginning. She said he was singing and whistling around the house, just happy.

This is not unusual for the impact this potent, powerful program has on people, when they are motivated and willing to come and work with the tools.

Young Adults

Many young adults are not as fortunate as Dylan to have been able to choose a profession they are passionate about. Despite his low high school score he had been able to talk himself into an advertising course at University. Many more young people simply drop out of school at the first possible opportunity. There is nothing wrong with that if they learn a trade that really interests them or follow their passion to work with animals, plants, machines or apply their incredible people skills. They may also be found in creative fields where no further study is needed and they will thrive.

However, there are a huge number of highly intelligent and creative young people who have fallen through the cracks. They are working in low-paid labouring jobs or any profession where they can get away without reading skills. Often disillusioned and not aware that there is another choice, they have given up their dreams and settled for a life filled with boundaries and restrictions.

I have met

- A young barista whose dream was to open his own coffee shop but, being overwhelmed with the tasks of legal papers to read, the bookwork involved and running a business, he gave up before he even started.

- A fantastic mechanic with similar ambitions to run his own garage. He actually started a Dyslexia Correction Program but didn't have the help from his parents or a girlfriend to continue. Without some support post-program it is very hard to keep up the work necessary to use the tools and add meaning to these abstract words.

- A highly successful builder who ran a big shop fit-out company with over $20 million turnover a year, fitting out specialty stores, hotels, designer boutiques and exclusive businesses. His company went into liquidation—in his own opinion due to his dyslexic characteristics: frustration, chaos in the brain, overwhelm, anxiety, lack of structure and the constant need to rely on a partner for all the tasks requiring reading and legal affairs. He has to find the time to do a program in the near future.

- I have worked with several young people with highly interesting and unusual professions: Colin was leading people through "out-of-body" journeys into other astral planes. He wanted concepts to understand our third dimension and also be able to read about them with more ease.

- Perry was a meditation teacher who wanted to study the "Gestalt Method" and needed additional reading skills to keep up with the course. He has since finished the studies and as a consequence achieved his dream.

A desire to study or change profession is the number one reason adults come to see me and work through issues. What often ends up happening is a far more life-changing experience that comes with the realisation of related issues that were never contributed to their dyslexia. That could be an issue with time, sequence, math, a lack of awareness around consequence, a compulsive need to always be right and many other issues.

Some adults come with a fear that people might perceive them as less intelligent or that their "bluff" will be called and someone might find out that they are actually dumb. That is not only a misguided fear but also a totally wrong self-assessment.

Dyslexia Test for Adults

If you are an adult and not sure if dyslexia is the cause of your problems, here are some indicators. Of course nobody has all of these traits and a lot of others won't be named. Some of the characteristics you will find in yourself, though:

1. At work, do you

- Work at a job that will hide your literacy difficulties or where you aren't required to read and write much?
- Work in a higher position that requires a secretary to write?
- Hide your literacy level from your colleagues?
- Become frustrated attending "boring meetings" and slower or orderly tasks—often feeling that you already have the answer and others are painstakingly slow?
- Get easily frustrated or anxious in new situations?
- Feel overwhelmed by new or unexpected tasks?
- Choose or prefer a visual, tactile or kinaesthetic career like: Designer, Architect, Engineer, Tradesman, Mechanic, Actor, Artist, Musician, Athlete, Sportsman, Builder or a Businessman with staff?
- Display a lack of concentration of difficulty to focus on one task, preferring to multitask?
- Pass on promotion to avoid having to write reports?
- Avoid tests, having difficulty passing standardised tests, sometimes blocking achievements or self-sabotaging?
- Consider yourself highly successful and driven—or an underachiever, not living up to your own potential?
- Come up with creative new ideas that are out-of-the-box?
- Try to avoid reading manuals, rather learning by doing, hands-on or demonstration?
- Watch a YouTube clip on how-to-do anything?
- See yourself as practical, street smart and a good judge of character?
- Make choices intuitively or instinctively?
- Display a sixth sense, or "read" people?

- Remember having struggled at school, with reading, writing, spelling and/or math?
- Rely on others to assist you, having become a skilful delegator?
- Make frequent spelling mistakes?

2. *At home, do you:*

- Have poor recall of conversations or sequence of events, often arguing about occurrences?
- Have a dyslexic child or children and sometimes see yourself in their struggle?
- Feel insecure or avoid reading to your own children or helping them with their homework?
- Get easily distracted, stressed, frustrated or overwhelmed?
- Appear to "zone out" and retreat into your own world?
- Play computer games or video games?
- Get told you mispronounce words, without realising it?
- Excel at sport?
- Have excellent memory of some events and hardly remember stories from your school days?
- Remember people's faces but not their names?
- Get accused of not listening?
- Find it hard to remember verbal instructions, especially lengthy ones?
- Avoid reading out loud?
- Read silently or speed-read?
- Find it easy to come up with jokes and situational humour?
- Find that comprehension depend on the subject matter?

- Frequently have to re-read sentences in order to comprehend?
- Quickly become tired or bored with reading?
- Rely on your partner for literacy skills?
- Like writing capital letters only or use poor handwriting to mask poor spelling?
- Guess at the use of punctuation marks?
- Find hard math concepts easier than simple math concepts?
- Have right-left confusion?
- Lose track of time and are either always late or obsessively punctual, finding it hard to estimate how much time passed?
- Lack self-esteem in certain areas of your life?
- Function poorly in stressful situations?
- Live rather disorderly or compulsively orderly?

All these traits are part of the same coin. Although on a wide spectrum, they still all indicate the same visual and creative strength paired with all the difficulties we hear so much about. It's our gifts that need to gain more attention and strengthening.

I have seen it over and over while working with countless adults that there is a lack of awareness of the positive aspects of their dyslexia. Paying too much attention to what needs fixing rather than on what is working so wonderfully can sabotage any effort to correct or ease the situation. Whatever we pay most attention to, we tend to get more of! Keeping that in mind, it pays to play with visualisation, with art and with creative focus. We play with them by using that medium to find answers to the puzzle of reading, spelling or anything that they would like to play at with ease.

Instead of fighting the emotions of anger, frustration, sadness or depression, we can sit with them, accept what is and what has led us to who we are now. Often anger comes up when adults realise how easy it can be to read and focus when they "get it." Anger that nobody helped them when they were at school or struggling all their lives. Anger at parents or school or friends. I let them sit with these emotions and make them realise that they have come to be who and where they are now with all their strength and perseverance and determination because of these struggles. Everybody has done their best and whatever the parents and teachers knew how to do.

Is it ever too late for adults to face their issues and correct their dyslexia? This is an account of a successful adult program:

Dr. Mike Perry is forty-two years old and has been working as a GP for ten years. He had been studying to become a dermatologist for almost as long. Most people would never suggest or recognise that he is dyslexic. The Board of his own medical profession didn't believe him when he suggested that dyslexia might be the reason behind having failed three years in a row to pass the final exam to give him the well-deserved specialist title. To prove him wrong, he was sent to Brisbane for testing. He tested positive for dyslexia (sounds like a disease, which it isn't, of course), which caused his superiors to suggest he'd give up any hope of ever passing the final exam and to just be happy that he somehow "fluked" to become a general practitioner in the first place.

Luckily Mike didn't take their advice and sought help instead. When I first met him and suggested that it was never too late and there was no reason why he should not pass that big final test, he became emotional and had the confirmation of what he had already known: He is very smart and it's all in place already—the information just needs to un-jumble and become accessible whenever needed. Having a client with this amount of determination, intelligence and motivation is almost like getting an unfair advantage. I was so excited to start working with Mike.

He decided to book in at the Retreat on the Beach where I usually work from and stay there for the entire week. On our first day of working together I had woken up early with an inspiration that I had never received before: The success of this program would involve more aspects than just adding dyslexic tools. Looking at the whole person would need to include exercise, a change of diet and weight loss, releasing any possible emotional blocks and working with special emphasis on medical literature. When I suggested this to Mike, he told me that he had just read the same suggestion in a book somebody had given him to bring along.

Being on the same page was a good start and we began the day with a one-hour walk on the beach, a dip in the rather cold ocean and an emotional balancing technique called "the Healing Code." I had taken the original idea from Dr. Alex Loyd, who had written the book with the same title and had added a Hawaiian prayer, called the Ho'oponopono. The powerful four sentences (I am sorry. Please forgive me. Thank you. I love you) are used like a mantra while at the same time the fingertips of both hands rest above four areas of the head that link directly to our endocrine system. The first position is above the third eye, the second one above the Adam's apple, the third one with the fingertips above each side of the head, at the end of the jaw bone, and the last position just above the temples next to the eyes. The entire procedure takes no more than six minutes and has a very calming and regenerating effect. It removes the fight-and-flight symptoms of stress from the body and gives our body the ability to heal itself—as only the body can. Alex Loyd had developed and used this technique to help his wife overcome a life-long severe depression and subsequently helped many patients overcome any kind of disease.

It certainly did the trick for Mike—he relaxed visibly and felt a new sense of ease and calm. On the second day when he did the Healing Code by himself, he told me that afterwards he opened his eyes and a ray of sunshine was peeping out between the clouds and a pod of dolphins was jumping out of the water. What a confirmation of being at the right place in the right state of mind!

And what a great foundation to start the new program. To provide breakfast was also part of my plan, together with all other meals. There was no sugar (only some fruit) and no carbohydrates on the table for the entire week, yet plenty of delicious organic food. We had Bircher Muesli with puffed millet and stewed fruit for breakfast, plenty of salads, Quinoa with roasted vegetables, fish with greens and many other wholesome meals. Weight was lost, energy returned, but that wasn't so amazing in itself. The best part was his realisation that all his focus had been on his studies for so many years, neglecting the most important assets of his life: his wife, his children, his health and wellbeing. It was great to witness the shift into balance. He realised that it wasn't even that important any more if he would pass the "blooming" test or not. However, we both had no doubt about his ability to pass the exam, which will not take place until June of next year. It will be his final chance to attempt it—and of course he will pass, if he chooses to go for it.

As far as his dyslexia was concerned the program was a breeze. Mike Perry learnt to generate a laser sharp focus point that allowed him to visualise everything he read and have full comprehension without having to ever read things over and over, like in the past.

His memory improved, when used in the way that was easiest for dyslexics to implement—in a visual way. All the many diseases in Latin terms and with all the symptoms had already been floating around in his brain, like butterflies that he couldn't quite catch or sort into the right categories, were finally coming together. Every group of skin diseases received a colour and a room in his virtual mind where it was placed and could be retrieved at will and with ease. Things that were closer to the skin surface had a place near the virtual windows of that room; others were in the darker areas. With clay models to originally support the words and add the symbolic meaning, it was later on just a visualisation technique that became like child's play for the clever mind of this amazing man.

I will never forget the last day of our five-day program. Mike's energy and the level of presence had changed completely. There was a new confidence around him that I had not seen before, a calm certainty that will without doubt attract the circumstances to him that he chooses to focus on. It is the same energy I see in people who have found their personal power. He looked at me and told me that he had received so much more than he had imagined—more than he could express. I knew exactly what he meant and look forward to hearing where this new knowledge and wisdom will take him in the future.

Working with adults is an amazing privilege—as without real motivation they wouldn't have made the call in the first place. They usually have not been persuaded by a parent or partner, but by their own yearning for change. The same is true for any child who is motivated and ready to take responsibility for their own learning.

Adults may have developed more "old solutions" and patterns that need to be dissolved, but they also have a highly functioning frontal lobe for higher reasoning and executive functioning that isn't fully developed in a child or young adult until they are about twenty-five years old. Knowing what we know now about the brain's ability to change at any time we can make full use of these abilities that are unique in us humans. Science has told us that it takes our brain approximately three weeks to form a habit, and with some motivation most of us can spare three weeks to embrace a new way of thinking and learning.

DYSLEXIA

E – EXERCISES for Dyslexics

To improve Reading, Writing and Spelling

In preparation for any exercise, not exclusively for the dyslexic learner, a good foundation is the key. Naturally this includes the obvious: good sleep, good nutrition, a clear mind that is uncluttered of thoughts and is not galloping in every direction. Often the latter is easier said than done. Thoughts seem to have a life of their own, seemingly secreted randomly from a mind we ought to have control over. Any form of meditation has been scientifically proven to have a positive effect on our brain and our learning abilities. Studies have shown a pronounced shift to the frontal left cortex which is the area that is associated with higher thinking and wellbeing.

Reading Exercises

Previous chapters have been describing many variations for reading that don't involve the "sounding out" of words, which has helped the auditory student but failed the dyslexic or visual learner.

Here is a summary of tips:

- Always start at the basic level—in this case the alphabet—to make sure all letters make sense and that the alphabet is known; not the alphabet song. Many parents assume that being able to sing it also means that their child knows it. More often than not, there are some letters that trigger in a big way and any word starting with such a letter might cause confusion. Often the reversal of b, d, p, and q is an issue or the sounds g, j—or the shape W, M—or an emotional connection to a name, etc. Have all letters, upper case and lower case, made in plasticine and mastered before reading can commence.

- Make sure the child/adult with dyslexia knows the meaning of the punctuation marks. Without it, comprehension will be distorted and sometimes misunderstood. Often children don't stop at a full stop and continue to read, meshing sentences together. If they stop, they have been taught to breathe, but fail to create a picture in their mind that ties the sentences together like slides of a movie.

- For intermediate reading levels, similar to a typical seven-year-old, choose a simple book and only read for a short time one letter at a time. Start by choosing a book or a text that is easy yet whose topic interests the reader. It is preferable to toss the book over your shoulder if it's too easy and move to something closer to the age range of the struggling reader than to step down. If a child can hardly decipher any of the words in the simple book, don't make the exercise about reading at all. Instead, ask her to just spell a group of letters and then, after a short pause where the right word might be known or guessed, simply tell the child the name of the word that she had just read. Only then can she be expected to read the same sentence again, this time only spelling the few words she still has trouble with.

- Always start with the spelling of each word, letter by letter, for about one sentence or more. It slows down the child's brain and helps with eye tracking, which is a good thing to start with but can get boring and tedious after a while. Then move to word recognition and after that to proper reading, stopping at each "stop sign" (full stops, question marks, exclamation marks). Any word the child doesn't know, ask for it to be spelled, without sounding it out. Then tell her the word. Reading out loud is not easy for any child, especially for the struggling ones. So we would never ask this task to be performed in front of the class or to more than one person. It is not designed as torture but simply an assurance that what is read is actually the same as what is on the paper. If you watch carefully you will notice how many small words are getting missed or changed. They are the ones without a concrete picture and will eventually need to be mastered.

- After each sentence or couple of sentences ask the child leading questions, e.g., how many years had he lived in that cave? What was the name of the younger child? Do you remember how often they had seen him? Who was that talking, when they say "he"? etc. Not only does it give you certainty that the text is understood, but it also sharpens the mind of the person reading, as the child becomes accustomed to paying attention to small details. This ability will also translate into more awareness in many other areas of schooling and life in general. It will help avoid the boring task of re-reading a passage over and over in order to get the full picture. So the slowing down will actually speed up the process in the long run. When the comprehension is getting better and better, there are fewer questions and interruptions necessary.

- Of course, reading by themselves is fine, too and will give them the enjoyment of getting into the story. The ten to fifteen minutes of reading out loud is more the exercise for comprehension and spelling. It will give you an indication of the improvement that happens all the time.

Writing Exercises

Sometimes it makes sense to start with the writing, even if it's only a dictation to somebody else. The idea gets across, it is a creative process that increases the confidence and nurtures the spirit of a child—and once they see the lines that they created, they may be much easier to read.

Most visual people have wonderful and creative ideas, stories worth telling and spellbinding suspenseful drama to impart. Unfortunately many of these stories never get written. As the saying goes, the richest places on this earth are our graveyards, with all these songs that were never written or sung, with all the stories that never made it into books or movies, where all the potential died together with the dreamer who never fulfilled his dreams.

I am convinced that many of the world's most famous and well-loved books were coming out of the creative visual brains of geniuses who would nowadays be known as dyslexics.

Do you have great ideas, all jumbled up in the brain, fighting for your attention to get them all out at once? Do people find it really hard to understand what you are writing about? Does it never look as good on paper as it did in your imagination?

Here are some ideas on how to help the stream of creativity flow in a better sequence:

- Regardless if you are writing for your own pleasure or an essay for school following a given title, start by pouring out all the thoughts, ideas, expressions, pictures onto individual pieces of paper. The small stick-it notes will do just fine for that task. On each little piece of paper, write a word, a phrase or even a short sentence, whatever comes pouring out of you. This is simply a download and helps clear the mind. Have as many as possible and be sure there is nothing left inside of you to the topic at hand. Example of a title: *"Would you rather grow up in a city or in the country?"* Example of individual notes: *"fresh air in country – more out-of school activities in city – better High Schools in city? – more time outdoors instead of in front of the computer – ride to school on a bike or horse – more friends to choose from in city – home-grown food in country – better job for dad in city – more helpful neighbours in the country towns – slower rural*

101

lifestyle – going to nightclubs better in town or city – can have a dog on the farm – animals – etc. etc."

- There are no right or wrong answers here, and this is just an exercise of wringing the brain out like a sponge to get every drop of creative idea and juice. After the downpour, read through the many notes and sort them into different piles. There may be the obvious country versus city piles, but also within them there are different categories. Lay the notes out, one below the others to come together like a sequence of thoughts that are now making more sense. *E.g., Pile 1: Country – 1ˢᵗ Category: Nature (fresh air, healthy environment, greenery, forest, lakes, fishing), 2ⁿᵈ Category: Lifestyle (slower rural lifestyle, more helpful neighbours in country towns, animals, riding to school by bike or horse, etc.), Pile 2: City – 1ˢᵗ Category: City Lifestyle (better job for dad, more money, opportunity to do ballet and dance, better sporting facilities, going to nightclubs, more out of school activities), 2ⁿᵈ Category: School (better High School in the City, more friends to choose from, etc.)*

- If an opinion wasn't already clear from the start, it will start to crystallize now and can be felt as well as seen in the amount of points in each pile. Now it's time to write the body of the essay or speech. The order or the chapters have already been laid out and can be cross-referenced with the opposing points. Make it interesting by combining sentences, by painting pictures in the minds of the readers and finding interesting words without repeating yourself. E.g., Instead of writing: *"I like the life in the country. The neighbours are friendly and helpful. I have a dog and two cats. I like my dog and in the city he would not like it."* you could phrase it: *"Having lived in the country all my life, I can easily see its advantages. The Simpsons, our neighbours, have helped build our house and I got my dog Sammy from their litter last year. Could I imagine living without Sammy? There is no way he would like life in a small unit in the city, where dad was offered a job."*

- Once the body has been written and the position is clear as to what you would prefer, it's much easier to write the introduction and the summary to a story. To involve the reader you can ask an interesting question in the beginning. You can tell them to "imagine" and paint the scene of the place you are living to get them to understand your decision and feelings.

- Many dyslexics have become excellent and prolific writers, not so much despite their learning disabilities but because of their amazing creative mind that evoked unforgettable stories that we are all privileged to enjoy:

- Agatha Christie, whose books sold four billion copies in one hundred and three languages, was dyslexic and suffering from dysgraphia. She described herself as an "extraordinarily bad speller" and couldn't remember numbers.

- F. Scott Fitzgerald, who wrote *The Great Gatsby*, was kicked out of school at the age of twelve for not focusing or finishing his work and could hardly spell. He is considered one of the greatest American writers of the 20th Century.

- Dav Pilkey, the author of the popular *Captain Underpants* series, was diagnosed with ADHD and dyslexia—he acted out as a class clown and ended up being a famous author and illustrator of children's books.

- George Bernard Shaw, a famous Irish playwright who won a Nobel Prize for Literature for *Pygmalion*, was dyslexic and ADD. He likened schools to "prisons and turnkeys in which children are kept to prevent them disturbing and chaperoning their parents."

- Jules Verne accompanied us on a *Journey to the Centre of the Earth* and *Twenty Thousand Leagues Under the Sea* and of course *Around the World in Eighty Days*. As a student he struggled at school and complained of a hard time to focus.

- WB Yeats is considered one of the most important figures in 20th Century literature and claimed that "several of my uncles and aunts had tried to teach me to read, and because they could not, and because I was much older than other children who read easily, had come to think, as I have learnt since, that I had not all my faculties." His father had given up teaching him and flung the book at his head. Although he eventually learned to read, he always remained a poor speller—yet received the Nobel Prize in Literature in 1923.

- John Irving, known for great novels such as *The World According to Garp* and *The Cider House Rules*, struggled at school, kept a diary of constantly misspelled words and was forever rewriting his work throughout school.

Spelling Exercises

Poor spelling is the one key all these writers have in common, apart from the obvious talent to enthral and engage us with their extraordinary ability to draw us into their imagination. They are all gifted in painting pictures for us, to let us take part in the emotions and lives of their heroes and heroines. I don't believe that poor spelling should stop anybody from expressing their talents.

However, sometimes the spelling is so inhibiting that not even a spell-check can offer help. Sometimes the embarrassment about their poor spelling ability does stop people from even picking up a pen. Sometimes the dreadful handwriting is only a disguise of an inability to spell and made the scapegoat.

The general approach to teaching spelling is the same as the approach to reading. The first method focuses on phonics—not only systematically but also explicitly. Systematic phonics programs teach letter-sound relationships and try to instruct in analysing and sounding out of unfamiliar words. The second method is the opposite approach—the "whole language" program. There words are not systematically pulled apart, as the focus is not the sound of words but the meaning. The idea is to surround the child with books that are read to with the assumption that they would pick up reading automatically. Guessing at a word from the context of the story should help the child to eventually pick up and enjoy reading. This hasn't proven to be the case.

Tests have established a better result with the first approach, which admits that early intervention is the key here. The best results for the phonic approach came out of kindergarten and Year One groups.

No third or subsequent options are presented by experts on dyslexia. Maybe a creative visual mind such as Ron Davis was needed to come up with a third approach that not only helps very young learners, but anyone with a visual or tactile approach to learning.

With experts in the field there is a general assumption that any word that is decoded is also understood. Therefore the easy words which they expect any three-letter word to be, should be understood and mastered at an early age to prepare for better spelling and comprehension of longer words for older children. Unfortunately this is not the case for most dyslexic children. Often the difficult words are understood and read while the short ones lack a picture and therefore a clear meaning. These words have to get a clear picture, which a dyslexic facilitator will help a child to achieve and truly master.

The English language contains a great amount of irregular spellings; there are as many exceptions as there are rules to spelling. Therefore decoding words phonically causes even more distress to individuals who don't learn by listening. They learn by seeing, by doing or creating.

Here are some tips to improve spelling, specifically for visual learners:

- Children usually bring home spelling lists, lists of ten or more words that they write every day of the week until that word gets tested on Friday's spelling test. Any word that still causes a problem or whose spelling is a hit and miss, there is a way to select these words and spell them with the alphabet letters that were create before (see reading exercises). These letters should be named like the alphabet, put in the correct sequence, slowly, one after the other and with a small space between two or three letters (depending on what makes sense to the child). For example: "fri end", "mis take", "regu la tion or reg ul at ion'", "ex cu se", etc. Then the word should get spelled forward, backwards and forward again. A mental image is taken while fully focused (it makes sense to have some tools in place at this stage, where a child knows how to gain or bring back their focus when needed). The child then closes his eyes and spells the word again, forward, backwards and forward again. Some children keep their eyes open and look at an imaginary screen on top of the ceiling or to their side.

  I once worked with a nine-year-old boy who was spelling "and" after making a model of the word. When it came to spelling it backwards, he noticed that DNA is also a word and asked what the letters stand for. We looked it up in a dictionary and found that it stands for "de oxy ribo nuc leic acid." He did that word in clay letters, with the little separations as above and knows the word to this day, forward and backward just as easily. Quite amazing, these kids!

- Later on or the next day, ask them to look at their mental picture if the word is still there and then write it onto paper or a whiteboard. The more attention and focus went into the initial creation of the picture, the better the word will be remembered long term.

- Start a list of new vocabularies or make a chart of new words learned each week and month to motivate and demonstrate a visual reminder of the success.

What can cause concern is a mix of instructions that is happening at school and at home after a correction program. If the school is on board and willing to incorporate the new learning style, not insisting on going back to phonic instructions, it will benefit the child. There is always great merit in partnering efforts to help a struggling student.

DYSLE**X**IA

X – X-FACTOR: DIFFERENT VARIATIONS

Who else lives on the Right Side of the Brain?

Dyspraxia

When I first met John I got the impression as if he'd been placed into his body by accident. Not only was his walk awkward and his eyes somewhere in the distance, his speech seemed as "muddled up" as his body movements. Not many children I had met were verbally dyspraxic as well as physically. Dyspraxia is one of the developmental coordination disorders, usually affecting movement and coordination.

Another area that was affected was his learning, naturally. His short-term memory was rather poor and so were his literacy skills. According to the medical profession, there is no cure for DCD (developmental coordination disorder), only coping strategies. I am not overly confident but find blanket statements rather challenging. The same way I don't agree with the generalisation that there is no cure for autism; I don't accept any statements and assumptions that confirm the current status quo of our medical and scientific model. The human mind has a far greater potential than we give it credit for—and to awaken our inherent self-healing or self-modifying facilities is my aim, not to "cure" anything or anyone. I don't believe we have the right to judge anyone's condition as needing to conform to an acceptable level or to fitting our box of what we'd like to see. However, if a child would like to reach another level of expression and find it too difficult or impossible to overcome their difficulties, I would do anything in my power to ease the process. This is done with passing tools to the child, tools very similar to the ones we give to our dyslexic children.

Ron Davis believes that the reason a person is "clumsy," as in the case of children with dyspraxia is the position of their "Mind's eye" in relation to their body. If the "Mind's eye" is ahead of the body, instead of behind and above the head, it causes a distortion of one's perception. Straight lines are perceived to be shaky or disrupted, which accounts for the need to hold on to a railing when walking down stairs, to add a sense of security before stepping on this "uneven" surface. As everything else is also not in the right relationship to the body, it is no surprise when the child stumbles into furniture or appears accident prone. The print on the paper is equally distorted.

To John it seemed like there were no straight lines in the books and he tried to make sense of the waves and the difference in the appearance of print on the right and left side of a page. In his case, the left side of a book was much easier to read than the right side. Even without the label, I would have picked up the symptoms at every step of the program:

- At the assessment I heard that there was a difficulty for John to learn to ride his bicycle, to balance on a skateboard which he still cannot do at the age of eleven and that he holds on to the railing when going up or down stairs.

110

- His mum reported delays in walking, articulating, colouring in, focusing; developing speech, handwriting, math abilities; holding cutlery, scissors; doing up buttons, shoelaces; following instructions and generally having a prolonged processing time and difficulty following instructions.

- When doing the alphabet, copying the letters from an alphabet strip, there was a distinct difficulty in forming any letter with a straight line, but even more so the slanted straight lines, such as in w and v.

- When it came to catching a ball, while only standing one meter ahead of me, it was a difficult task, even while standing on two legs. Standing on one leg was almost impossible. John's coordination and balance was definitely suffering as a result of his difficulties.

- Physical activities such as walking, running, jumping and climbing were compromised.

- John's language problems seemed to me like an extension of his sequencing troubles ... the sounds were not in the proper sequence and were either jumbled within words or the words within a sentence.

- Holding a pen seemed awkward and unnatural, but we didn't need to go there—at least not for a while.

- Additionally I picked up that there was no left-right differentiation, leading to a poor sense of direction.

- I needed to put instructions into simple terms to not confuse him or add too much information to remember correctly.

- There were difficulties in tasks requiring sequence or time-management.

- There were some similarities to the Asperger clients I had worked with, especially when it came to sensory overload, low muscle tone and a high level of anxiety.

- After about three hours of working, fatigue set in, not surprisingly due to the body's need to his difficulties with any physical task trying to coordinate and pay attention to instructions at the same time.

According to Ron Davis, making sure the orientation moves into the right position in relation to his body was the first and most important task. It was not that easy to achieve in John's case, as the instructions needed to fit his level of ability to perceive language.

Dyspraxia may affect language, physical movement and learning, but it does not affect the intelligence of a child. John certainly was a bright young man and obviously frustrated about his inability to show his true potential. Consequently he was having trouble making friends and enjoying most of the activities of children in his age group.

Although about 10% of the population is dealing with some kind or degree of dyspraxia, this condition will only be picked up in 2% of the population, four out of five of them being boys.

The only way John was able to establish a different orientation was with a tactile approach which we often use with very young learners or dyslexics who are kinaesthetic rather than visual learners. The instructions being shorter and simpler, additionally being shown on a model rather than just explained in words, helped John to follow and successfully implement the procedure. Although hard to tell if the Mind's Eye, which naturally is invisible, is at the right position, the effect of it is easy enough to detect. When John was able to stand on one leg without shaking and wobbling, I knew he had done it! What normally happens in one day, did take a couple of days—but what a difference after that. It may not amaze an outsider to see a balanced human being but, believe me, I was excited. John's face lit up!

Perfect balance leads to a different perception of reality. It means that everything moves along with it. Any sense that gets aligned—in our case the sense of balance—draws all other senses into natural balance too. Visual perception was aligned: the letters shaped became straight lines instead of overlapping shaky lines. The ocean that can be seen from my office showed up as straight lines, as if drawn with a ruler, John noticed. After a week he felt confident enough to walk up and down the stairs without even holding on. He could catch not just one ball standing on two legs, but he managed to catch two balls while balancing on one leg.

It slowed him down enough to perceive sound in the sequence that it occurred and slowly but surely altered the way he spoke. Although it took longer than I had anticipated, the outcome was nothing short of miraculous. A great deal of credit goes to his mum, who spent many hours following up and reinforcing every step that we had put into place, with total trust in the process.

When I called John the other day, he was telling me about the birthday party he had been invited to—which in his eyes was a far greater achievement than any learning improvement. He had made friends.

Hyperlexia

Hirdai means "heart"—and the thirteen-year-old boy from Sikh origin was full of heart and spirit when he showed up at the centre with his parents and his sister. I had never before worked with a child who was hyperlexic and really looked forward to the new experience. The family had come all the way from Perth to work with me—so I had no opportunity to meet and assess Hirdai prior to the week we worked together. His mum had explained the long journey they had already travelled to get from severe non-verbal autism to a high-functioning autistic individual showing much intelligence and awareness. However, his hyperlexia was keeping him from progressing further. Seeing young Hirdai sitting across from me, with his turban and beard that made him appear far older than his thirteen years, extremely well behaved and attentive, I vowed to do my very best to not disappoint their blind trust and faith in me.

There had been many interesting phone conversations with Hirdai's mum beforehand. Coming from a highly educated family, where academics are obviously valued, she wanted to know all about my education, university degree and credentials. Having heard about her son's special sensitivities and strength to pick up on people's energy, his spiritual inclination and intuition, I simply asked her if he'd relate to my degrees or my level of empathy and presence. After a short silence on the other end of the call, Harmeet agreed with me and we went ahead to book the program.

The Davis training is rigorous and emphasizes the fact that we are facilitators, not teachers. As facilitators our role is not to instruct and inform. Instead we provide strategies and tools to awaken the inherent creative spark and use it to learn differently. This takes sensitivity, intuition, calm and presence to hold the field for these amazing individuals and sometimes act on sheer inspiration to uncover another hidden layer of the talent under the difficulty.

This boy was another opportunity to work from a point of "not knowing" and although using the same formula, still come up with a personalised approach that would end up being the key to unlock the comprehension of this lovely boy.

Hyperlexia shows up as:

- A great ability to read well beyond the age or average reading level, yet without the understanding of the words read.

- In Hirdai's case I heard him read an adult book of great complexity without making a single mistake. Of course it didn't surprise me that he couldn't tell me what he had read. But when I asked him to read a simple children's book, suitable for an eight-year-old, he still could not comprehend anything he had been reading. Despite the precocious reading ability, the communication skills were lacking as much as the comprehension. The way the words were expressed reminded me of autistic children with echolalia, the repetition of words like echoes. His voice lacked rich tones and variations.

- Intelligence, showing an average or above average IQ and above average decoding skills. Some evidence coming from fMRIs show that hyperlexia may be the neurological opposite of dyslexia. I did not see that in the functioning of Hirdai, as there was an obvious link with dyslexia, in the difficulty making sense of words without obvious pictures.

- Most children that show signs of hyperlexia also present as autistic or on the spectrum towards autism. As such hyperlexia is often coupled with other autistic traits: problems with social interaction and making friends, sensitivities, fixations, need for routines, etc.

- Hirdai presented most of the above autistic symptoms, as well as the inability of hyperlexic children to answer questions of "why, how, who, what, when, where?"

His parents' hard work in the past made it easier for me to work with Hirdai. He worked tirelessly, never wanting to stop—I had to insist on short breaks, pretending they were for my own benefit. Although he didn't speak much, he could—after thinking for a while—answer in short and halting sentences, usually in a flat tone of voice.

I proceeded with him in combining our Dyslexia Correction Program with the Autism Approach. In order to have pictures for the small words, he made the alphabet and we mastered some of these short yet very common words. Additionally I slowly introduced life concepts, such as "change," "consequence," "time," "sequence" and "order" over the space of the five days I had with Hirdai.

With every day and with every concept there seemed to be more of the boy present and aware. As much as the focus exercise helped him in his ball catching, it also got him into his body. He looked more focused and he walked with more purpose. He even started to contradict his mum, which absolutely amazed her. He has always been such a good boy, she had told me—and I explained how important it is for an individual to start objecting. It was the beginning of being an individual. We all go through these stages, some more intensely than others. We call it the "terrible twos" for the young children when they become oppositional. A lot of autistic people haven't gone through that stage and Hirdai was starting to go through that phase, which may not be so pleasant for a parent, especially when the two-year-old is thirteen.

Finally we started the reading process, with one of the early chapter books. I stopped him at every sentence, sometimes even after a comma and asked him all these questions that usually a hyperlexic child has trouble with. "Who was speaking, when they say 'he'?" "Where did the boy play with his car?", "What was the name of the man next to him?", "Where is the dad?", "Which was his favourite car?"

Being almost impossible to answer, the replies were mere guesses in the beginning—and usually wrong ones. Yet the longer we persevered and the more of the small words that were actually on the page were becoming images and models, the clearer the meaning formed. Eventually the entire page was like a movie in Hirdai's mind and he told it to me in his own words. It came as a big surprise to his mum as it showed real insight and clear individual thought and reasoning. Even the tone of his voice had more depth.

I have talked to his mother again when they returned from a holiday in India and she told me how amazed his relatives were when seeing him again like this. He had never been more alert and interactive. Of course he still has a long way to go—and hopefully will return to finish more of the concept work to conclude with the awareness of relationships. After knowing himself he will find a way how best to fully participate in life. Only then does it make sense to look at making friends.

Asperger's/Autism

My experience of working with a dyspraxic, dyslexic, Asperger's boy from Western Australia:

After I had finished my Davis Autism Training a couple of years ago, I had the fortune of being contacted by a mother from Western Australia about helping her twelve-year-old son, whom she was homeschooling at the time. Highly religious, she told me that after fervent prayers, she had received the message from Jesus that I'd be the best person to work with Jared. She arrived a month later, with her son, who wasn't able to look me in the eye, to say more than "I don't know" and as he stumbled up the stairs, one of the dyspraxic signs, my heart went out to him immediately.

After my refusal to use Jared's own bible and a video recorder to film everything, we could start the process that would take us two full weeks. I usually don't mind reading whatever the client brings along, and I have no problems for my clients to read the bible, but this was a different case. This boy had never ever read anything else— nor was he supposed to, according to mum. I asked if she still agreed with our initial aim for the program: to help her son to fully participate in life. She finally conceded that there is more to life and since his main goal was to go off to school, instead of continuing with homeschooling, I was allowed to proceed with a children's book (of course not my beloved *Harry Potter*, as in her eyes that was Devil's literature).

In the beginning I gave Jared lots of tools to gain a stable orientation, a lot of release and relaxation for all of us, clay work and field experience. It was difficult at times, working with someone looking over your shoulder and pulling you aside for "using the Lord's name in vain," every time I said, 'Oh my God, what a beautiful model!"

Every day Jared and I would go out and discover the world, finding evidence for the concepts that we were installing in his mind. Concepts such as Change, Consequence, Time, Sequence, Order and many others are part of the Autism Program. He relaxed a lot when we were out, maybe also because it was the only time that mum wasn't controlling his life to the last detail. Every day, as soon as we were back and anybody would ask him, what we did or what he had for lunch or who he saw, his answer was always the same: "I don't know."

One day, however, something strange happened. The two of us had gone for lunch to the beach, bought a sandwich and were about to proceed to a bench to eat it, when a seagull swept down and picked a big chunk out of Jared's lunch, which he had just held in his hand. He looked a bit shocked, but said nothing. When mum asked him afterwards what he had for lunch, his automatic response came up "I don't know" and then I interrupted him and asked if someone tried to steal his lunch? It was like a light bulb went on in his head, he became animated and alive, told mum all about the seagull who took his lunch, that it was an egg and bacon roll, that Barbara (me) had forgotten to put money into the parking meter, etc.

From that moment on he improved in leaps and bounds, started playing with his cousins, where they were staying, talking, reading and generally becoming more and more individuated. He started to participate in life, mum started to relax and speak to him in softer tones and I started to believe that there was indeed some intervention from above—a seagull is close enough, right?

I never forget the day I saw him for the last time, feeling quite emotional about the good-bye and as he was about to walk through the gate, I asked him, if he'd miss me as much as I'll be missing him. He looked me straight in the eye and said, "No, Barbara, I won't miss you. You are in my head now." At that he pointed at his head. What a beautiful boy!

DYSLEXIA

I – Imagination and the Brain

How the Dyslexic Brain differs from the Neuro-typical Brain

Many scientific studies have been conducted into the different areas of the brain that light up when people read or learn to read. They found that dyslexic readers use different pathways to non-dyslexics readers. That in itself is not new. For most non-dyslexic readers phonetic decoding is the best way to learn to read and comprehend.

For the dyslexic brain, however, brain scans suggest that the information flows along rather different pathways on the right side of the brain. It mostly bypasses the left hemisphere, where the sounds are translated into words by the non-dyslexic children. Nobody disagrees with these findings. What differs are the interpretations and conclusions that most experts draw from this evidence. The approach that is recommended in almost every instance is an emphasis on phonetic decoding through intensive drill and training the brain to improve its left hemispheric areas. The Davis Method for correcting dyslexia is one of the few strategies that emphasises creative, meaning and focus based ways to acquire the necessary literacy skills. It draws on their right-hemisphere strengths and abilities, rather than trying to force non-verbal visual individuals into left-brain dominance.

I have come across interesting research, described in *Overcoming Dyslexia* by Sally Shaywitz, carried out on dyslexic adults whose reading development had been monitored since kindergarten. The group chosen had a history of severe reading impairment in early childhood. The interesting part of the study was that some of the individuals still struggled in adulthood, a group they called "persistently poor readers," while the others improved significantly in their high school years and turned into accurate readers with strong comprehension. Using functional magnetic resonance imaging (fMRI) the researchers tried to evaluate the reading tasks of both— the improved and the non-improved readers, as well as a control group on non-dyslexic adults. The finding: highly improved dyslexic readers showed an increased activation of the right temporal areas as well as the frontal lobes on both sides, but no more left brain activity than in childhood. The poor readers showed a similar brain picture than non-dyslexics, with activated left posterior and left temporal areas lighting up—yet without the reading abilities of the non-dyslexics control group. They tried to rely solely on "sounding out" and memorising, lacking comprehension and word analysis skills.

Interestingly, the improved readers bypassed that area, displaying advanced vocabulary and comprehension, having discovered strong compensatory strategies.

Phonetic decoding and auditory processing support are highly effective when applied to non-dyslexic readers, but fail to achieve the desired positive results when imposed on a dyslexic child. The research from Yale University has demonstrated that using the left-hemispheric pathway, through phonetic processing, often diminishes, rather than improves the dyslexic child's reading capability.

Any teaching method is geared to building cognitive skills, the meaning of words, analytical thinking, reinforcing the natural talents inherent in the dyslexic student.

Changes from the brain's perspective

How to retrain the brain?

I am sometimes asked by parents how to get their children off the computer, especially if they are totally hooked on some online game, like World of Warcraft, war-hammer or many other virtual reality games that capture them and enable them to live an alternative reality.

Especially children who fail to thrive at school and get acknowledgement for academic achievement, seek to excel in another area—any other area. It is a basic human need. However, the choices for these outlets vary greatly, from a healthy approach to sport, music or any other field of the arts, to a less healthy gravitation to technology, by creating an online persona. Many children (and adults) fully identify with their character and the games they play in the virtual world.

I feel the anguish of their parents who cannot relate or find room in the world of their children any longer. When the children are young, we are often still seen as figures of authority or even parental heroes. In these cases it is naturally much easier to reduce the times spent on the computer or in front of TV, to encourage alternative talents and distractions.

Sometimes we are going through rough times ourselves, experiencing traumas of our own through losses, changes and huge challenges. An already sensitive child will then retreat even further into the alternative realms of some game—and we are almost relieved that we can deal with our own issues, not noticing that these children slip silently out of our lives.

When they are adults, how can we regain access into their lives? Usually there is no or little motivation to change from their perspective. What would be the one area of their lives where we have leverage and can insert our influence and encourage an opening and change? If there is even a glimpse of hope to get their cooperation or motivation to become more involved in what we call our reality, it will be worth pursuing. As without a want from them, we are fighting a losing battle.

The more we push, the deeper they will retreat.

If, on the other hand, there is a will to change, there is a way to reform the habits.

What we are trying to do is to retrain the brain to branch from negative memory patterns and create new neural pathways to view life from a wider palette or range of experiences.

Unfortunately, our brains have a tendency to remember the negative things that happen to us much more clearly than the positive ones. That tendency may have originally served us well, when, for example—many centuries ago—we were hunters and gatherers, and were sampling berries that made us feel sick. That memory, enhanced, would have served us well to not eat poisonous things again, to watch out for danger in the environment, dangerous smells or animals—a great warning signal. However, this negativity is not serving us so well nowadays.

Our areas of consciousness exist in the frontal lobe of our brain, yet the neurons extend well into the back of the brain. These more primitive or primeval parts of the brain pay attention to whatever happens in the outside world. When you have a negative thought, the rest of the brain is going to react as if that thought was a real threat happening on the outside.

How to reverse engineer our brain?

Even if our positive thoughts are nothing but a fantasy, a future vision that has not yet happened they are able to stimulate the motivation centres and release dopamine, our happiness hormones. It will make us excited about life, jumping out of our skin with energy and joy, and doing all the work required, driven by that self-created carrot at the end of the stick. Our reptilian brains are unable to differentiate between a reality in the outside world and a thought or feeling we "invent." Both are seen as equally real. This is the crux of our power to change.

How useful are the visual ability and creative gift of those dyslexic picture thinkers becoming when seen from that brain perspective. Actively participating in a different version of life turns visualisations into powerful change agents.

There are many ways to train the brain. We never listen with all our brain; we just devote a tiny bit of consciousness from the frontal lobe to a new way of thinking and being. The majority takes place in the subconscious, or the unconscious part of us.

An exercise to awaken to the NOW

As much as we are orchestrated by our subconscious mind, we cannot ignore its needs for pleasure. We don't have to let these pleasures control our life, but we can use them to awaken into the present moment. Even small pleasures (like tiny bits of your special comfort food, a quick run, hot bath), enable us to experience present moment awareness: Mindfulness.

You may want to try it, as there are many ways to experience a simple pleasure that still has the power to shift you into the driver's seat of NOW. It could be a conscious deep breath, a yawn, a stretch, an awareness of the pressure of your buttocks on the chair, or the feet on the floor. If you touch your hair or face ever so softly and slowly, or gently stroke one hand with the other, you cannot help but shift out of your mind and into your body. What happens in your brain at that time: it produces more dopamine, our feel-good hormone. When totally relaxed and present, any pleasant thought can bring a smile to your face and attract more people into your life, more pleasant experiences, more softness and healing. It releases the tension that we so often hold unconsciously.

This small exercise will translate to the quality of your voice, when you talk to your child, the ability to sit and listen without being negative, nagging or critical.

When you hold a positive vision, after stimulating the pleasure centres or by actively participating in joyous thoughts and feelings, someone else's brain is resonating with it; they too will feel good and without knowing why, they want to be in your presence. It's what science calls "Neural Resonance."

The opposite, "Neural Dissonance," is the law of unattractiveness, where it is not pleasant to be around you. We can get this dissonance in certain places, around people and things, without being able to rationalise it. It's just a feeling—or did something negative take place in these surroundings or lives?

Science is able to prove this quite extensively and people who are able to shift their emotions at will have displayed the ability to change the quality of their DNA—and also of somebody else's DNA. The findings go back to early research by Russian scientists in the late 19th century and have, amongst others, been proven by the Institute of Heart Math. In their experiments they used individuals trained to control their emotions (coherence-building techniques), hold a test tube with somebody's DNA sample in it. DNA spirals are wound much tighter when emotions are negative and looser with feelings of love, peace, joy, etc. The winding or unwinding of the DNA sample proofed again and again the relationship to the emotion that was displayed.

Gaining Access to the Subconscious Mind

Any change we desire is only possible, if we are able to gain access to the subconscious. Not only is that part running the show, but it is also the area where our emotional blocks, our mind viruses and past conditioning keeps having a hold on us. No amount of willpower can penetrate our subconscious programming—at least not in the long run.

There are many tools and practices to be discovered that have the ability to remove these culprits, so that we can employ ways to reprogram and change with new patterns of thoughts, feelings and emotions. I have come across a wide range of ways to access our deeper areas of consciousness: Hypnosis, EFT, Theta Healing, the Healing Codes, and Brainwave Entrainment, sound therapies, specific questions, visualisations and many other ways.

We are supposed to use our consciousness to create our reality. Instead, our lives and expressions have become word-based, automatic inner speech, originating or spoken in a habitual and unconscious manner. Instead of creating wisdom and a life of choice, we are living shallow echoes from a past experience, memories of past traumas and childhood assumptions. Therefore, words are rarely the best way to solve problems, as they originate from the subconscious pool of data.

Try to interrupt that unconscious chatter and place your attention into the moment, the presence.

Mindfulness to change old habits

Be mindful of which part of your brain is firing and if the result is not pleasing or useful, try to shift out of your negativity. If you find that difficult, then create a little mantra for yourself that can serve as a "first-aid" kit until you have sufficient time and the right tool or practitioner to help you shift the major blockages. A mantra could be, to tell yourself "I breathe in love, I breathe out peace." Simply saying that a few times can shift your energy to a more peaceful place. Some words have deep and profound meaning and an ability to rewire your brain and even change the genetic blueprint of your brain cells.

Have you seen the movie *Avatar*, when they get on the horse and connect the long braid of hair with the horse's tail and they become one? That's what a new habit creation could possibly look like in the brain. A new pattern creates new neurons that grow new telomeres, connectors to other neurons.

Most successful entrepreneurs are practising some form of

meditation or mindfulness to increase productivity, joyful activity and to increase their awareness and output.

Do you know which kind of activity or imagery most fires up our brains? Just watch the advertisements and they will confirm the neuroscientific findings:

In neuroscience there are also three specific images that motivate us humans to the greatest action:

1. Loving, romantic, erotic interaction
2. Comfort food or drink
3. Money (research has found that even the subliminal flashing of a coin for twenty milliseconds can become a powerful motivator).

Our lower pleasure centre always wants more. Its functioning is selfish and unless it is balanced by Higher Consciousness, it is difficult to break free from a cycle of desire.

Patterns of addiction are not only in many of my clients, but in the majority of people. Anxiety, intense worry, fear or self-doubt usually stem from a past memory that replays scenarios on a repetitive loop.

We are not necessarily addicted to substances, but more often to behaviours, experiences, pain, unhealthy emotions, pleasurable ones, and anything else that we fail to stop doing or experiencing.

We are either conscious creators or recyclers of our collective past. Are you living or being lived?

I have also seen this over and over again with clients who are not experiencing a full appreciation of their potential. They can—with the aid of such a vivid mindset—experience injustice and persecution from every new teacher, every new school and it literally makes them sick. They are born to create, but haven't learnt how to.

Both the positive vision of a brighter future and negative anxiety of an uncertain future are just illusions. In order to shift old habits, we have to break them in the present moment, as only here and now we have access to our potential.

After shifting undesirable habits, they need to be replaced with more useful ones.

The best way to help a creative child—any child is creative—to make that shift is to listen actively.

Did you realise that the word SILENT contains the same letters as the word LISTEN?

Listening with compassion to someone else's views, in a relaxed and mindful state, extraordinary things happen. When speaking to your child, slow down your speech, relax and share from a deep level, the child's comprehension will go up, and they will feel with you. Compassion results and communications shifts from confrontation to a common ground of understanding and cooperation.

When we walk slower, speak slower, eat mindfully and savour the flavours, we boost our immune system. We can meditate with every word we speak, in every action we take. Not many people have the time to sit in meditation for hours, so mindful action has replaced the stillness to some degree.

Nowadays a lot of children, teenagers and young adults are already experiencing anxiety or even depression. Latest research has found that mindfulness, acceptance and awareness are the most effective ways to solve it. By not focusing on the problem, or making it wrong, we allow the feeling to be there, and depression decreases. Any trauma, when watched without attaching judgment to it, diminishes.

Mindfulness—the ability to pay attention to the present moment— creates new neurons and enhances the frontal lobe of our brain. We can effectively diffuse any situation when we learn to watch, observe and release. It is our judgment that makes it right or wrong.

I believe our school system would greatly benefit from adding some mindfulness strategies to the curriculum, as these are infusing change in most areas of our lives.

DYSLEXI**A**

A – ADD/Attention Deficit Disorder & ADHD/Hyperactivity

There may have been a lack of attention on the activity at hand but there certainly was an overabundance of attention on everything else that was going on in Sophie's life. She was not hyperactive, but hyper-alert. Every tiny detail beckoned her eye; she asked me why I had a green rubber band around one of the legs of a small cupboard in the corner (a fact I hadn't noticed before) and was intrigued by the picture of a yellow canary on a boy's bandana as shown on a book cover. Her ears were equally busy, picking up the song that was playing on a car radio that was driving past and surely many other stimuli that Sophie didn't have time to comment on. There were many other stories competing to be told, memories that came up with each new impression and stories she had heard from others. The sharing was hardly edited before it poured out; words became almost a compulsive stream out of a very bright but overly active mind.

ADD or the hyperactive variation known as ADHD often go hand in hand with dyslexia, but not always. Sophie came with a diagnosis of ADD and in Sophie's case there was no obvious link to dyslexia. Her reading was average to good—but her school work was nevertheless hugely affected by her inability to pay attention to the teacher for any length of time. There were many comprehension issues and other difficulties related to the inattention rather than confusion around language. Life can get pretty tough for children who cannot reign in their mind to obey their desire to be present in class—or in life. They often feel bored and frustrated about mistakes that they don't know the reasons for. Their thoughts seem to have a life of their own, galloping away at the slightest distraction.

The program we decided to go ahead with was not a traditional Dyslexia Correction Program, but a Davis Attention Mastery Program™. The aim of that will be to help Sophie to focus at will, with self-regulatory tools and help her to develop solutions for her own learning and behaviour.

Like dyslexic children, Sophie too is prone to disorient. Her mind is wandering and the place she is perceiving her reality from is distorted. The level of distortion depends on the reasons and to what extent she will be distracted. It depends if she is bored, tired, overwhelmed, overstimulated or simply amusing herself with her ability to become aware of more information in the environment than other people would.

In this state of distraction, information will either be changed or missed altogether. Sophie does get into trouble at school; there are disciplinary actions, detentions and letters to her parents. Being as bright as she is, Sophie has found ways to not get caught and strategies to camouflage her mental journeys. What disturbs her mum most are the stories and excuses that seem like lies and ways to get out of performing tasks.

The issue that Sophie wanted an answer to was her frustration about constantly getting into trouble, often without knowing the cause of it. The program does include the understanding of concepts, one of them being the concept of "consequence."

Not being focused means that we miss vital concepts, building blocks for understanding fundamental laws. I am not talking about our legal system, but basic natural laws. These structures cannot be negotiated, they just need to be understood and experienced on three levels: as an understanding (by observing them), as knowledge (by experiencing them) and as wisdom (by causing them).

When Sophie modelled and made sense of the concept of "consequence" as something that happened because of something she did or didn't do beforehand, it made a lot more sense. Clarity came in and understanding on a very deep level. A few weeks prior to our program she had been sent to the principal's office yet again. She said that Paul, who sat in front of her, had it in for her and always wants to get her into trouble. He had called her by a name she hated and she was the one who was punished. When we broke down the scenario into a sequence of events, it made a lot more sense, that hitting and scratching would be seen a worse offence and that there are other strategies of reacting to annoying behaviour and words that only have an effect when the person reacts.

Not only did Sophie see the model from the chronological perspective of a timeline or events, but also from the different perspectives. She became an observer of her own behaviour and that of anyone else. She then put herself into the shoes of the boy, of the teacher and of the principle and parent, and finally into her own shoes. By exploring other options and responses she was able to establish a new set of behaviours to supplement the one that always got her into trouble in the past.

New knowledge can override old behaviour patterns. It is important to test the field after that and see if it works in real life. A part of it is the observation of others. One of the comments Sophie made that was interesting was that she has now become much more aware of other people's choices, the useful ones as much as the ones that sabotage their efforts.

In contrast to dyslexia, where confusion about letters and the lack of meaning in certain words or symbols can trigger a confusion and with it the disorientation, an ADD or ADHD child gets triggered by the environment, by stimuli or as a means of entertainment.

Where dyslexics draw blank pictures with words such as "if, by, so, nor," a child with difficulties of putting the attention on one subject or keeping it there will miss important life lessons. These life concepts are missed or misinterpreted and lead to confusion and insecurity.

While dyslexics may only disorient for a fraction of a second or minute while trying to make sense of the symbol, the disorientation in a hyperactive or attention deficient child could last for hours.

A dyslexic child may not show any signs of trouble until school starts or until they are first confronted with the written word. ADD shows already in the early development of a child. Hyperactivity signals are present early and usually show up as soon as a child can walk and run.

What leads to learning challenges in dyslexics often leads to life challenges in ADD/ADHD children. The feeling of being out of control is a debilitating burden to live with.

Spending all this time out of their own range of focus may easily lead to develop signs of dyslexia almost as a by-product of their mental distractibility. How can a child be expected to learn the extremely challenging task of learning to read and write with only a fraction of focus in comparison to their peers? Often the most intelligent children achieve this task despite all the challenges—and can do so out of sheer boredom with what seems to them extremely slow learning counterparts.

Have you seen the movie about the creator of Facebook, called *Social Network*? Its creator, Mark Zuckerberg, may have more Asperger traits, but there is one scene I really loved. He was sitting in negotiations about a payout to his former friend and partner, but his attention was everywhere else which clearly seemed to annoy and frustrate everyone. He made a comment that even with a fraction of his attention on the issue at hand he'd be able to get it and draw conclusions before the others would have reached them. It reminded me so much of these bright individuals we diagnose as ADD.

Clearly they don't need help to increase their IQ—as it probably exceeds my own. The objectives for Sophie and all my ADD clients are to:

- Receive tools to become the masters of their own mind—to become orientated and use their Mind's eye to their advantage.

- Become confident and skilled in continuously reigning their mind in when it is required to be on task.

- Explain to them the reasons for their spontaneous disorientation and the problems this can cause them at school and in life. They need to understand the role they play in creating their own impulsivity and inattention.

- Gain deep awareness of the concepts that make up the natural law, concepts such as "change," "consequence," "time," "sequence" and many others. They need to be presented in a structured format that will be supported by life's experiences. Whatever doesn't make sense will be rejected or objected to.

- Personalize these concepts to create a new order of behaviour which has to replace the conduct that fails to support their growth and learning. The motivation for each change has to be clear and evident—the gain obvious.

- Supply support for social interactions, on how to make friends, keep friendships and interact on the same energy level that the friends' activities require.

- Help these individuals to "dial down". They are usually able to do anything a "normal" child does, but a on a more intense scale: they may appear louder, faster, more boisterous, more in your face. There is nothing wrong with that except that it often stops them from making friends, or being part of activities that are happening on a slower pace.

- Support the individual need and confidence. Despite their high intelligence, self-esteem is usually not very high and their academic achievements don't reflect the level of the intellect.

In fact, one of the official definition of ADHD is:
Underachievement and poor social skills despite normal intellect and quality parenting.

Problems with attention, over-activity and impulsivity often impair social relationships. 4-6% of school-aged children and 2-4% of adults carry the official diagnosis—many more remain unaware or unidentified.

We don't need to focus on labelling everything and everybody but if there is a way to extend help to those who are struggling to understand their world, help cannot come soon enough.

Unfortunately there is an increased tendency to medicate these children or for adults to self-medicate with drugs, alcohol or other ways to overcome their emotional difficulties for a short period of time.

Sophie is going into high school next year with an increased awareness and level of control. She will continue to make mistakes like we all do, but she will understand the consequences and keep learning new ways and strategies that can help her. Her inherent intelligence will serve her more and more, instead of tying her into knots like the lead of an untrained puppy, out of control and not able to serve her in the long run.

She realises that she is not stupid and the newly developed self-esteem helps her to make better choices. As she has realised that there is an excess of energy in her, even without being hyperactive, she has taken up netball and soccer, which the parents hadn't encouraged previously. It helped her also to make friends and the gain the appreciation we all need to thrive and feel part of a group. It had the unintended side effect of increasing her patience and level of tolerance. Nowadays not everything has to happen at once and it's okay to lose and train harder to achieve another outcome. She is a happy girl now.

Why the Right Brain for the Right Time?

The title of this book stems from my deep belief that we are living at the cusp of a new era. We are entering or have already commenced the age of energy, beyond and impacted by the era of information. This is not implying that there ever was a time when energy was not at the core of everything … the only difference is that we are becoming more conscious of this fact. As time appears to be speeding up, or simply more creation happening in the same time frame, we are confronted with the result of our manifestation very quickly. It causes "angst" and overwhelm in many people but for those who are aware of it, this phenomenon presents a great opportunity.

Everything "Quantum", from Abundance to the Zero-Point field, have become buzz-words in many people's vocabulary; the Matrix has replaced our purely mechanical world view. Consciousness is seen as the new universal currency. Ever since the Law of Attraction has tempted us to become co-creating forces to shape our life experience we have been told how to best create a new reality. What we had perceived to be the "reality of life" has consequently been shaken at its core. So we don't have to accept the cards that life seemed to have dealt us?

Any system that is promoting the increase of our abundance and happiness involves visual conceptualisation. Not only do we picture the reality we desire, but we are asked to feel it with all our senses and to believe it as if it was already real.

Dyslexics think in pictures

The dyslexic mind is pre-set for visualisation. If pictures and the creation of our reality are in our invisible realms first, then dyslexia must be the perfect pre-disposition for the creation of a magical life. It certainly has helped many very successful dyslexic individual achieve success by anybody's standard.

Then why are so many of them struggling, in poorly paid jobs, lacking confidence or even in jails?

An ability to generate our own reality doesn't differentiate or show a preference to one type of outcome over another. In other words: We are mostly creating by default. The very things, images, feelings, fears or desires that occupy our waking hours are becoming manifest.

If we are fearful of living in poverty, losing our job, getting sick or any other phobia, fantasy or fear we may entertain, we are creating exactly that what we fear, hate, love—especially when a lot of emotional force is behind it. Of course we think that we don't want to be poor, broke, sick or lonely. Yet the very words "don't" or "not" are picture-less. All the mind sees is the image, either the image we want, or the one we want to avoid. Not only is it the picture that will attract those circumstances into our lives, but the more intensely we are trying to push it away, the more it will persist in our lives.

Taking this well-proven and publicised manifestation approaches into account, wouldn't it make a lot of sense teaching our young generation how to avoid the pitfalls of victimhood? I believe it's time to stop repeating our cycles of lack, blame and guilt. Instead we have to instil the tools of creation into the hand of each individual and emphasize the responsibility that comes with the power, responsibility not only for their own lives but also for the use of these tools for the common good.

For most of my life I had been instructed by others how to behave, what is the right thing to do, feel and think. Our media shapes the way we see the world, selling negativity and shock value, manipulating us into believing that the world is a dangerous place, that most people are evil or victims and hypnotizes us into believing in the fears that are motivating our drives to buy certain products. Our subconscious, already beaming with fears and lies, readily accepts more of the same. Awareness of our mind viruses or ghosts is the first step to break out of this vicious cycle. Yes, a book may draw one's attention to a lack mentality that doesn't serve us. But it will not be enough to become an engine for deeper and lasting change.

There has to be some inner work—a learning that doesn't happen overnight and needs focus, persistence, attention. It has to become a driving force in its desire to shift our lives to another level. This new vibration will become the engine for any image we are holding that needs to be drawn like a magnet into our life.

Being fun and creative, this will be child's play for any dyslexic person and a wonderful challenge for anyone else. How it can help us parents to get out of fixing our children—and playing with new ways of empowering ourselves instead, will be the content of my next book, which greatly focuses on my own journey out of anxiety into an exciting and rewarding life.

Dyslexics are Daydreamers

Have you ever been told to get your head out of the clouds and into your books or your work? Many people believe that if only the child would focus on their work, they would be fine. Not only is this well-meaning advice easier said than done, it also can be stopping one of the most vital and undervalued experiences: Daydreaming!

There is an entire study done on the ways how daydreaming can increase one's IQ by as much as forty points. It is based on the fact that we are using the right hemisphere for daydreaming and by adding the left side of our brain to express what we see, it becomes a powerful whole-brain approach, allowing the brain to work in a more synchronized and efficient way. The spoken or written recall of one's daydreaming material adds a vital aspect to the exercise. It makes it more conscious, giving an activity that may be a bit chaotic the shape and focus to retrain the brain.

This seemingly simple approach nevertheless has a long-lasting positive effect and creates neural pathways between the two hemispheres. The technique, originally developed by Dr. Win Wenger, one of the world's foremost researchers in the fields of intelligence and creative problem solving suggests the following steps to permanently increase the average person's IQ substantially. He calls the process Image Streaming:

1. Close your eyes
2. Be aware of the stream of images running through your mind at that moment
3. It's fine if they seem random, unclear or unorderly
4. Describe out loud everything you see or become aware of
5. If you see nothing, just say, "I see darkness. Black."
6. As soon as something fades into view, describe it "Now a beach comes into view" … or whatever happens
7. Describe also what you feel, smell, touch and hear. All senses can and should be a part of it.
8. Are people coming into the picture? What time of day is it? Does it feel hot? Do you feel sand between your toes? Hear waves or smell salt in the air?

The pictures you see whenever your mind wonders and wanders become movies of the subconscious mind. It's our natural ability and is a gift we can all use or develop. When first all we see is darkness, it won't take long to develop the ability to either see or to actively participate in the act of visualisation. The other natural ability we all have and our minds engage in is description. Description is a conscious act and happens in the left brain hemisphere, developing our ability to put our pictures into a sequence, where time and order are required. As we heard before, these are concepts that are sometimes lacking in a dyslexic learner—or perceived in an altered way. Concepts such as change, consequence, time, sequence, order and others are vital to integrate in order to successfully work with the entire spectrum of our brain. They are usually more developed in non-dyslexic learners, who sometimes lack the creative abundance of the picture thinkers.

Some people have actively switched off their ability to visualise as it may have caused them trouble in the past, regardless if it used to be their strength or not. For them to reconnect with this aspect of self is often a wonderful addition and provides higher problem solving skills, better intuition and inspiration.

Daydreaming without the boundaries of creative visualisation or descriptive expression to make them conscious often has no more value than entertainment and the escape from boredom, confusion or frustration. The person may as well be asleep.

Dyslexics and brain gym

I teach juggling to all my clients, on top of playing with the Koosh balls. The Koosh ball exercises—throwing two balls underhanded, catching them overhead, while standing on one leg—are highly undervalued in their ability to create and maintain focus. By throwing the balls to either side of the person, the mid-line needs to be crossed, adding the benefit of creating or travelling the neural pathways between the right and left side of the brain. I have seen school grades improve by several grades simply by persisting with this exercise on a daily basis.

Not everybody has a person available at all times to play Koosh balls with and learning how to juggle has added a skill anybody can master with practice. In fact, most children learn it faster than I did. They start off with one ball, throwing with one hand straight in front on their body and catching it with the other hand. Without focusing on the hands that throw or catch, it becomes so accurate and easy, that it's soon time to add the second ball. While one is up in the air, the other one gets thrown and caught with alternative hands. Koosh balls are easy to catch, as they have these rubbery strings. However, they can also be changed for proper juggling balls. Eventually the budding juggler is ready for three balls. Starting with two balls in one hand, one in the other, the excess ball goes up first and can be caught with the other hand after releasing the ball that is there, so one ball is always in the air. As with any activity, this is far easier to learn by practising than talking or writing about it. Get someone to show you or watch it on YouTube to get the hang of it.

Juggling is known to increase the IQ, but so are many other mental exercises, mind games, quizzes, mind mapping, computer games and memorising tricks.

Dyslexics and memory
This may well surprise some people who heard that their child's short-term memory is very poor: Dyslexics are perfectly capable of memorising feats. I am convinced that the majority of geniuses who memorize entire volumes of Yellow Pages, several decks of cards or who play chess simultaneously with twelve opponents are in fact picture thinkers. They may not be called dyslexics, but they are living

on the right side of the brain. They may also be called Asperger or savants or autistic, but they too have a strong right-brain dominance.

I have heard and seen the tricks they use in order to bring up the right number or recall every detail in the right sequence. Although not all methods are the same, the majority of them use images, yet images in sequence.

There is a movie attached with a clear sequence that never alters. It might be walking into one's own house and having objects like the deck of cards in different rooms, in groups of three. There are people, objects, activities and images combined to recall a proper order.

People who play chess with several people simultaneously "see" their opponents in different rooms in their brain, together with the chess boards.

With my clients I make a very personal movie, personal to their own place, their way to school or work and incorporating the daily sequence at school or workplace. These images have numbers and they never change. They just get superimposed with the knowledge that needs to be learned. It could be the multiplication tables, it could be history or geography facts or the diseases that my doctor client needed to recall. What seems to be a complicated procedure to explain is child's play for the visually inclined. It's fun! I had one child remember every multiplication table this way—in a very short time.

Dyslexics and the Heart

Improving one's mind and intellect are greatly valued by society. Schools are rewarding it, parents are proud of their offspring if they show intellect and our grades are measuring and judging the student by their ability to recall knowledge.

In my opinion this is a big mistake, keeping our abilities in the 10% or less brain capacity. We are putting our attention on the improvement of the left side of the brain, away from the right side: our heart. There is a strong link between the heart and the right brain. Both are present moment dominant, feeling or seeing states, intuitive and wise. Fantastic in itself, it becomes even more useful when in a whole brain pattern, where the organisation and structure of it helps to think more clearly, make better decisions and have less stress.

After having talked about ways to train the brain to synchronise these two hemispheres, I would like to focus on the heart. After all, it has the power to shift us out of our small lives and open us to a much wider field of possibilities. Change is a paradox. It may take time, yet only takes place in the present time. A shift into "now" happens when dropping into your heart space. Visualising dropping a pebble into a pond is one way of letting that happen. It stops your thinking mind. In fact, if you try to think or analyse if the shift actually happened will signal that it hasn't. Thinking will be replaced by feeling, sensing, being. It's a becoming aware of yourself in the present moment, with all the emotions, feelings, pains or pleasures that may be in the body at that moment. Planting an intention in the space between thoughts, an intention that is present before you "drop the pebble" allows its appearance in your life. The key word here is *allow*. There is no effort involved, no neediness of a particular outcome, no willpower either. It is an act of listening, rather than doing.

Wise leaders are able to combine their spiritual life, the meditations, prayers and working from a heart centred place with action—inspired action. The heart is the driver; the brain or mind serves it well. Dyslexics are often heart centred—making decisions based on feelings at any present moment. Wonderfully attuned to the heart through their right brain approach, they may, however, lack the action part (every desire is just another imaginary journey) or fail to consider the logical consequence of that action (making impulsive decisions that end up being poor choices).

Dyslexics are catalysts to change

Children are a wonderful catalyst for change, but a lot of us make the mistake of trying to change them, rather than ourselves. A child that struggles at school needs help, without doubt. On the other hand, that child needs to desire change, have the motivation to go through it and take responsibility for its transformation. Then change is empowering and lasting.

What they don't need is somebody who is trying to fix them or constantly points out what is wrong with them. The energy of the adult is far better spent on providing a supportive environment, where the focus is on the abilities and gifts of the child. There is always room to change ourselves, leading by example instead of improving undesired habits in others. Only questions will get an agreement or cooperation to get help. Questions establish a possible motivation.

I have had a very interesting client recently—a male adult in his early forties who taught me so much and became a catalyst for my change. The program had started out badly when the wonderful food and diet plan I had so cleverly devised was thrown off-course by a big fat roll with peanut butter on the first morning. My gentle reminder that we had agreed to follow a sugar- and carb-free week was badly received. I learned that my assumption that losing weight would be a good idea and foundation of a successful program was not really an agreement, as it was not reached through questions, but a suggestion. He didn't need my advice and I really shouldn't have assumed to know better.

Yes, he did want change, but the change I had offered was based on my past experience with dyslexic clients. It turned out that the change he was really seeking had nothing at all to do with his difficulties to write essays or study design. In fact, it turned out that to study wasn't even his main goal, but merely a security to fall back on if working in this profession didn't pan out. There were other issues that surfaced during the week and addressing emotional blocks, anger management, the sequence of his goals and the boundaries for an overactive mind replaced the initial reading and writing goals.

I had an opportunity to work on a variety of unexpected matters that bubbled up and found it very inspiring. I discovered that I couldn't think myself into or out of certain situations; I had to simply hold the space and see what solution presented itself. Once the outburst of anger at being asked to model an objective in clay led to a wonderful opening to facilitate the use of EFT (Emotional Freedom Technique). There is no point teaching EFT to someone who doesn't experience the emotion that needs to be released. Rating his anger at eight it was great to see it diminish in less than ten minutes to zero. What a wonderful tool this is to not suppress or ignore emotions. Although we ought to feel them, we may not want to entertain them for a longer period of time. To feel, acknowledge and then tap it out will not only offer relief in the short run, but lead to longer periods without angry outburst. The charge gets reduced and equilibrium takes its place.

Have you ever bought into an angry outburst of your teenager or reacted hurt or upset at what seemed to be aimed at you? I certainly had done that in the past, not realising that it wasn't against me at all. How do we find out what is really going on in their lives? It always goes back to asking good questions that are not offensive and then taking the time to listen to the answer. Listening involves the heart and the mind, it involves silence and the child will have the chance to unravel himself. No advice or judgment, very few words, an occasional question is needed. That way you will be sought out, as you will be the one that empowers them, not yourself.

FAQ

For my final chapter I have asked my friends, former clients, their parents and teachers to identify questions that they have or something that they wish they had known when they turned their initial challenge into a journey for themselves and their child.

I was overwhelmed with the feedback and support I received.

Here are the questions:

I think my child could be dyslexic. What are the symptoms and how can I be sure?

That is really a main question—and as much as it's easy to point to a long list of possible symptoms, it will depend on an assessment to be sure that dyslexia is behind them. They are only indicators, after all—and what we as Davis facilitators test is really the predominant learning style of a child or adult, if or how a visual or kinaesthetic learning style might affect their performance at school or the workforce.

If a child does show a non-verbal learning style and has obvious challenges, we can also determine if our approach will be the right one for them and if they are ready to change. Change happens when responsibility is taken for it. Ron Davis always points out that in order to be responsible for anything, we need to have the ability and willingness to control. If they show the willingness, we provide the ability.

The symptoms also depend on the age of the child.

Some of the many different indicators that your child may present at the preschool age are difficulties to:

- remember names, even their own name in writing, mixing up names (spaghetti/pasgetti)

- pronounce words correctly (my son couldn't pronounce the R in "run" and similar words)

- put clothes or shoes on the correct way

- learn to count, or read a simple group of letters

- Move with confidence, often clumsy or accident prone, and showing difficulty with gross motor skills (catching, throwing, skipping, etc.), which would indicate more of a dyspraxic tendency

- follow instructions, especially long ones

- sit still, listen, pay attention, etc.

Some of the indicators at primary or high school may be:

- Initial excitement about school dwindling, resulting in stressful days at school, coming home exhausted, often not having eaten anything

-Appearing bright and intelligent, but unable to succeed at school, even though trying hard

- Fast thinker, fast talker, but often slow to read and write, or unable to do so at year level

- Creative ideas for writing, but trouble putting in the spaces between words, spelling correctly or using appropriate grammar, not using punctuation marks

- Relying heavily on the pictures in the book, guessing the words

- Zones out, daydreams, exhibits a distorted sense of time

- Great difficulty in sounding out words, or understanding phonics

- Spelling or writing correctly one day, but not the next

- Trouble reading the small words, often more so than big words

- Good problem solving skills and can show a lot of attention in areas of interest, but difficulty to focus or remain focused at school, easily distracted

- Right-left confusion, and/or sense of direction

- High IQ, but poor self-esteem and a tendency to cover up their limitations

- Highly creative and artistic, showing musical, mechanical, mathematical aptitude

-Profound visual memory, often seeing the big picture, rather than the detail or a slower sequential process

- Spatial strength, organisational weakness, trouble with concepts of times, sequence and order

- Sophisticated sense of humour or class clown

- Tendency to omit words, skip lines, substitute or guess words

- Poor handwriting, trouble holding a pencil correctly

- May appear hyperactive, disruptive, or frustrated

- Confusion with shapes and number patterns, as well as mathematical symbols

- Difficulty with concept of time, telling the time, or guessing how much time has passed

- Active mind, but easily distracted, often to avoid the task at hand

- Finding it hard to memorize lines, poor working memory, generally to remember things

- Anxious, confused, displaying emotional outbursts in frustration

- Imaginative, with a pronounced sense of satire and intuition

The list could go on.

Can we avoid the 'label' dyslexia when talking to my child?

"Please don't use the word dyslexia when talking to my child," a well-meaning mother asked me before assessing her child. In the past, that is exactly what I used to do. Trying to pretend that there is no problem present, nor a solution necessary, just a slight adjustment.

I fully understand, when parents want to protect their children's emotional reality, or are trying to boost their fragile self-esteem. However, in the past ten years of working with these individuals, I have learned that this does more damage than good.

Parents and therapists that keep reassuring the children that they don't have a problem may rob them from a solution to eliminate their difficulties.

It gives children a false perception that often leads to a false interpretation of their challenges: "I must be stupid," being a common one—and nothing could be further from the truth. Often these conclusions stop the motivation necessary to resolve the learning difficulties and to take responsibility for their own learning.

When I talk to a dyslexic child and do point out that they are dyslexic, indeed, I also explain what it means to be dyslexic, how many advantages there are in having a big-picture mind and list the many brilliant people who share the "label of dyslexia" (from Einstein to Richard Branson). In just about every case, learning that they are dyslexic is a relief and finding out that this is not at all a disability, but a different learning style, additionally empowers them to accept the benefits and take responsibility for any changes they are motivated to make themselves. All they will need is some tools and strategies to do so.

Once dyslexic, always dyslexic? Will my child grow out of it?

That is a wonderful question and certainly a valid one, if we look at dyslexia from the point of the challenges that many children are facing at school. I truly believe that the gifts far outweigh the difficulties and will become more apparent in the later stages in life, often after school, at university or at the right job.

Although children don't "grow out of it," as much as they don't grow out of being creative or intuitive, they learn to use the strengths of their mindset, choose the areas they excel at and grow in confidence, when they realise the advantages they have over others.

The worst case would be to shut down their creative, visual abilities in an attempt to "cure" or "fix" dyslexia, making them feel wrong. We can and certainly should help provide tools for them to cope, but always bearing in mind that any help ought to create self-mastery and empowerment of the individual, not another crutch.

So the short answer is: Yes, once dyslexic, you will always be dyslexic—thank God for that! The world will catch up to your brilliant mind very soon. You are at the right place right now.

Is there a cure?

Dyslexia is not an illness; nor is it a disability, even if it appears to be that for many individuals, when they struggle and despite working harder, seem to stay stuck. Dyslexia is a different learning style—and as soon as there is a cure for an outmoded teaching style, many of the dyslexic blocks to learning will be cured too. The dyslexic thinking style enables them to view things in a different way, capturing the whole picture rather than working through a slower sequential process. So there is no need for a cure, but there are ways to bring out the gift of the non-verbal picture thinkers, to enable them to use the powerful creative mind set to their own learning.

Why do dyslexic children find especially the early school years so difficult?

Most dyslexic children are not diagnosed before going to school, and many not at school either. The most common difficulties often are not an issue in early childhood. They surface at school. Interestingly, the first words we have to read are non-picture words. Fifty-seven of the sixty words on the Essential Spelling List 1, 2, 3 are without meaning for a picture thinker. They are the two- and three-letter words, prepositions, pronouns, articles, adverbs: in, for, by, he, the ... For visual learners they are so challenging, as they lack meaning. 75% of the English language consists of these abstract words. Without certainty, often guessing through reading material, they are usually grasping for some kind of coping strategies. Finding these solutions may help them through school, but unfortunately these same solutions become compulsive coping strategies.

How do children perceive their school experience in hindsight?

I like that question—and I do pose it a lot to my older clients or former clients. It's interesting to me that there seems to be very little recollection. Maybe it is human nature to zoom out of traumatic experiences and by not getting consciously affected it seems to diminish the pain and anxiety. However, it does come at a high cost, often a tendency to get out of challenging life situations in general. Some children tell me that all they hear after a while of listening to a teacher, especially a "wordy" one, is "blah-blah-blah." Another common response is that certain basic knowledge was either never taught to them (grammar being one area) or without them being present. These gaps add to the confusion in later years.

Is dyslexia only affecting the performance at school or in other areas of their life?

Dyslexia affects every aspect of the individual's life. It is often thought of as a difficulty with literacy; however, it is not limited to school issues. On the downside there may be a low threshold for frustration, confusion, problems related to directions, short-term memory, emotional sensitivities, telling time or issues with time management, order, or putting their thoughts and ideas into words. A low self-esteem may cause poor judgment of peer groups, a tendency to favour virtual reality computer games or excessive obsessions. Sometimes it leads to health issues or other secondary manifestations of the problem of not coping. However, viewing the world from many different perspectives gives them the advantage of finding creative solutions in everyday situations, great abilities in artistic, creative, imaginative, humorous areas of life and very creative solutions to their problems.

How does dyslexia impact relationships? What is it like being married to a dyslexic man or woman? What are the challenges and positives?

It can range from lots of fun to lots of arguments. Having at the root of dyslexia certain difficulties with order, sequencing and timing, it can be frustrating for partners, as they often end up being the ones who keep the structure in place. They do the banking, the organising, the letter writing and other tasks to facilitate life, while the dyslexic counterparts add the fun, creative ideas and often excel at their profession. It might be the profession that absorbs them and distracts them from participating at home as much as their partner would hope for. Having such a vivid mindset can lead to misunderstandings, things they swear that they have already told you might have just happened in their mind. Understanding their mindset helps you to know that this is not done in malice. It certainly is never boring being married to someone who is dyslexic. You never know what is around the corner.

My grandfather is dyslexic, my father and my brother are dyslexic. Does it run in families?

From experience with hundreds of clients in the past, I would say that there is a genetic component to dyslexia, as 95% of the individuals I have worked with had a member of the family who was either diagnosed or showing the symptoms of dyslexia. However, having a genetic predisposition to dyslexia doesn't guarantee that you will develop it in life. I am not convinced either, that the environment we grow up in doesn't have an equally important role in the development of a dyslexic mind.

Is this the era to be dyslexic?

Wonderful question! If ever there was an era where these right-brain thinkers were to thrive, it would be now. Our world gets more visual all the time. We cannot cope well with the "infobesity" (the information overload), the increased speed of creation, the solving of problems with our linear way of thinking. It certainly seems to make sense that people who are visual, intuitive and creative are better equipped to come up with solutions to many of our major environmental, social, economic, energy and lifestyle problems today.

Is it cool to be dyslexic?

That surely is an individual question I wouldn't even dare to answer. I personally think that I am slowly getting more dyslexic, which is good news. I am striving to have a balanced brain, having access to both sides of the brain, depending on the task at hand. I have always thought of dyslexics as being cool, as I like individuals who don't fit into a box.

Why does the public still view dyslexics like aliens and fail to realise their talents?

I think that comes down to education. There is very little awareness in the general public, unless a member of their family is affected. Teachers are not taught special education more than a few hours during their training. Not knowing what they deal with, and being overwhelmed with too many children and too many issues already, they cannot be blamed for feeling frustrated with these children. They are not allowed to use the "dyslexic label" either, at least here in Australia, where officially, dyslexia has been removed from the diagnostic manuals ... and replaced with a wide range of different labels with lots of acronyms: ADD (attention deficit disorder), ADHD (attention deficit hyperactive disorder), ODD (oppositional defiant disorder), OCD (obsessive compulsive disorder) ...

Can you have varying degrees of dyslexia?

Oh yes, that is all dyslexia really is: a variety of different ways to cope with disorientation. There are no two dyslexics who display neither the same degree nor the same symptoms. Some dyslexics are only showing the positive aspect of it and hardly any literacy or numeracy difficulties—and would never even receive a dyslexic "title." They may not love to read and when reading, just leave out the little "boring" words (which is a sign of dyslexia, as they are having difficulty comprehending abstract words that don't bring up an image).

However, being as intelligent as most of them are, they still get the zest of the text and find coping strategies to cover up any difficulties. Others distract from a varying lack of understanding by becoming the class clown, the bully, the daydreamer, the chatterbox ... anything really helps them better than a feeling of helplessness, of not being in control.

Can dyslexics have problems in numeracy, rather than literacy?

Absolutely! And it has nothing to do with reversing the 6s and 9s, or of the numerals 43/34. That may also be an indication, but often the math problems are caused by a lack of understanding basics and missing foundations. Without the concepts of change, time, sequence and order, math is built on shaky ground. Once the pillars of math have been established and math is taught in an appropriate manner for visual learners, they usually not just improve, but start loving math.

A student also needs to know the reasoning and the objectives behind a mathematical problem. That creates the motivation to change in the first place.

I am currently writing a book on Math specifically for dyslexic individuals.

My child has been diagnosed as being dyspraxic? What does it mean?

Dyspraxia in the past would have been called chronic clumsiness. It is not always associated with dyslexia, because it doesn't necessarily affect literacy or numeracy. Often it affects auditory perception and children with dyspraxia are seen as being accident-prone. There may be other symptoms associated with dyspraxia, like poor handwriting, poor eye contact, a need to hold a book on an angle in order to read, different visual perception of one side of the page to the other. The handwriting is an obvious give-away. Dyspraxia can prevent someone from opening the neural pathways associated with accurate perception. A part of the visual perception seems to be blocked, which leads to lines not being seen as straight—or an inability to draw certain shapes accurately.

Unless these neural pathways are opened, an approach is only a forced attempt and not a permanent one. If a client feels dizzy and out of balance when I ask him or her to stand on one leg, I know that disorientation is most likely the culprit. The Mind's eye tends to be in front of them, rather than behind their head.

Distorted perception is something we can fix, but it takes a professional approach and persistent, diligent work afterwards. Dyspraxia affects motion and balance and only shows up in about 10-15% of dyslexic children.

Are there practical measures parents can take to improve the lives of children with dyspraxia?

Absolutely! I would recommend that the disorientation is tested as well and a more stable orientation established, before the exercises are applied. A persistent follow-up is vital, as new neural pathways take time to become established. Parents are the best providers to follow up daily with the ball exercises that would have been shown to them, as well as balancing and centring procedures.

How important is regular treatment versus a one-off intervention for dyspraxia?

Sometimes it is too difficult for parents to stay on track with the follow-up and it is always of benefit to see a specialist to rekindle the importance of some exercises. When we see parents for support training, it is often an overwhelming amount of information and not everything can be remembered.

Can these measures of intervention for dyslexia or dyspraxia be taken at any age or is it best to start early?

Yes and yes. There is no limit to the age when disorientation can be corrected, so that dyslexia is just a talent, without the associated struggle. The same applies for dyspraxia, as a new point of perception allows the elimination of the symptoms of misaligned balance and motion. However, when a child is very young, an intervention is there to prevent future issues, rather than correct them. On the other hand, I have had people in their sixties and seventies do amazing programs and completely change their lives. It all depends on the level of motivation—and often adults display a high level of responsibility and motivation. They have struggled long enough and are ready to take change seriously. I personally find that adding another modality, like EFT or the Healing Code (as also discussed in this book) to an adult programme counteracts negative past conditioning and accelerates a positive outcome.

As a parent, how can I best support my child in their learning, if they show difficulties?

After I had read *The Gift of Dyslexia* by Ron Davis, I had a much better understanding of the level of difficulty that my son was experiencing. It gave me compassion and a different paradigm to a situation that had previously caused me great concern. I relaxed in the knowledge that this can be corrected and also that there is a gift inherent in all these different problems. Apart from being educated, it also helps to support their confidence and help them to learn differently. If you don't have a Davis facilitator handy, you can do a lot of the exercises from Ron's book yourself. I am sure there are other modalities out there that can be helpful, often from an energetic viewpoint. These children are very sensitive and react rather well to alternative healing approaches.

The "fixing" professions, unfortunately, often focus only on the negative symptoms and try to add what is lacking. Seeing that these children are not very gifted in auditory processing, they tend to focus on phonics or phonemic awareness, which is similar to trying to teach an eagle to swim or a monkey to fly.

These children find it extremely confusing to have to sound words out as the same letter could have several different sounds, which makes no sense to them whatsoever. I have seen children burst into tears or feel nauseous when having to sound words out. The Davis method uses the right side of the brain to make sense of the words, without a need to sound them out, which is a left-brain activity.

I am a teacher and don't know how I can help the children in my class who show signs of dyslexia.

Again, like for parents, it comes down to understanding the mindset, embracing their differences, rather than putting tags on them that usually don't apply. They are often perceived as lazy, as they may be able to do a task one day, but not the next. I have heard teachers use this as a reason, that it can't be dyslexia, because I know they were able to do it yesterday. That exactly is the point. When dyslexics are focused, not in a state of confusion and disorientation, they demonstrate a higher level of ability and competence. When tired, confused or distracted, all abilities go out the window, together with the child's mind.

Another word that is not useful is "concentrate." It makes people become tense and achieves the opposite of what you want: focus! Focus is born of ease and placing one's attention to one area. If done correctly, focus is only a breath away and an important tool for the mind to return to the body, even if things aren't easy.

I have given the books by Ron Davis (*The Gift of Learning* and *The Gift of Dyslexia*) to teachers, but I doubt that many have actually read them.

As a teacher, what can I do with children who are hyperactive and distract the rest of the class?

Discourage the use of stimulants, such as Ritalin, even if it's tempting. There are healthier and more supportive activities that would help them.

When a child displays signs of hyperactivity, being forced to sit still and not move makes them nauseous. It's the closest to a feeling of seasickness. It's not just in our mind, but there actually is biochemical change happening too.

Children with ADD and ADHD display higher levels of the neurotransmitter dopamine. Disorientation shifts our perception of time and increases the dopamine output, and having an increased amount of dopamine around the synapses of the brain, the "internal clock" speeds up. Naturally, time in the classroom seems to be excruciatingly slow in comparison. Instead of using discipline to force them to sit motionless, encourage an activity when you see that happening. It could be as simple as running an errand, giving a note to another teacher, accompanying another student to the sick bay or anything you can think of. Movement, stretching or any combined class activity, like playing with Koosh balls is great to help them and synchronize the energy of all children.

170

Koosh balls (the rubbery, stringy toy balls) are a fantastic tool that many teachers use already. For additional benefit, ask your students to throw and catch while standing on one leg, throw them in a sequence to different children (teacher to Mary, Mary to Dean, Dean to John, John to Patrick ...) and after a while, reverse that sequence, which keeps them totally focused and on task. Ask them to catch overhead, like an eagle would catch a mouse, while throwing them underhand, with the balls next to each other, in one hand, so they arrive at the catcher's eye level simultaneously. Throwing the balls to either the left or right side of their head has the additional benefit of mid-line crossing, when they catch the two balls. Very young children (approximately up to the age of eight) have trouble catching the balls overhead and find it easier to catch with both hands stretched out, palms facing up.

How do I overcome my own frustration as a parent with the system, and with my child's inability to cope in that system?

Unfortunately we cannot change the system; we can only help a child to cope within the system. Our education system is changing, but very slowly and not always in favour of the struggling children. The level of support in school varies too; some are more accommodating than others.

Sometimes the schools that seem to welcome diversity and have a lot of support in place end up being the worst choices. They create classes for "special cases," where fifteen to twenty-five children with a variety of issues are pooled together and they end up triggering each other. The unhappiest children I see actually come from these classes. Not only do they find it hard to cope in the class setting, but additionally with the stigma of being in "special-ED" and the bullying that often comes with it. I would love to find a school that focuses entirely on the gifted, visual learner and tailors the curriculum around the strengths of their students. Please let me know if you have found one.

Does the condition change over time without any intervention?

I don't know if the word "condition" is helpful here, as again it suggests that we are dealing with a disease. Yes, there is dis-ease here, but not a pathological one. I have talked to many adults who have never received any help or intervention during school or after.

What I have found is that they have become masters of home-grown solutions. Often they tell me that they used to be dyslexic, but not anymore. No, they still don't read much, and if they have to, they read a text several times to fully understand it. Or I have adult clients read a page, almost without a single mistake, but when I ask them what they read, they would tell me an entirely different story. They are almost surprised that I point that out, as normally people wouldn't notice. So, great storytelling helps. Having a secretary helps. Having a wife who takes care of these "things" helps. Spelling is often an issue, writing as well, but their intuition, intelligence and resilience compensates for many shortcomings. Often intervention is only an option if there is a danger of losing the job, or they are seeking a higher position which requires them to write reports, or they have children who want to have dad read a story to them at night.

Generally, learning problems don't disappear over time, without any intervention, but more coping strategies will be used and cover up the difficulties.

What jobs are perfect for dyslexics?

Dyslexics excel in jobs where their gifts can shine. These visual, creative individuals develop great talents in areas such as problem solving, spatial awareness, lateral thinking, mechanical skills, drama, music, the arts in general, inventing, building, strategic planning, storytelling, architecture, athletics, sport, engineering, etc. They are often great leaders, too—like Richard Branson.

I find that dyslexics are individuals outside the norm or "the box." They are the ones who are at the very top, the leading edge or the ones in prison. Unfortunately an estimated 70% of prisoners are illiterate, too.

Luckily we are living at the age of information and energy and our society continues to move towards more technology and creativity based professions.

Dyslexics make great business leaders, architects, teachers, builders, writers, mechanics, artists, designers, actors, engineers, sportsmen, doctors, IT specialists, programmers, musicians … the list goes on.

How many people in Australia are illiterate?

A study from the Australian Bureau of Statistics (2007) has rated the literacy and numeracy skills of 9,000 Australian's on a five-point scale.

The result:

46% of Australians DON'T have the literacy and numeracy skills to participate effectively in present-day Australia, testing on Levels 1-3.

17% of them score on band 1, which makes them illiterate or very poor readers.

When testing their "life-skills," Level 3 is considered the minimum needed to effectively cope in today's life in Australia. The participants had to read financial documents (like workplace agreements), health instructions, newspaper articles and similar everyday numeracy tests: calculating change, understanding percentages of a sales item or the interest they are paying on the mortgage.

In no way is the result skewed by non-English speaking migrants; in fact, they are generally placing a higher value on learning and putting more effort and money into their offspring's education. If you think, this statistic rates us poorly, you are wrong. Australia rated pretty well, being placed fifth in an overall worldwide PISA ranking. I have read a more recent study that suggests that we have sunken far further on the international PISA ratings scale.

Is there a link between literacy and income?

As mentioned before, dyslexics are found outside the box, so their level of income is often well above the average, but in many cases well below.

Statistically, there is a $200 income difference per week just between a level 1 and a level 2 reader. An improvement in a child's reading skill might be a rewarding investment.

What help can I expect from the schools or the Board of Studies in term of study aids? What do I have to do for my child to get special provisions, so they are not disadvantaged at school, Uni or Tafe?

Approach the school as soon as you realize there is a problem with your child for all exam or assessment tasks. Ask them what they will need to enable the student to get special provisions throughout their high school years ... do not leave it to the HSC year.

Special provisions can include:
-extra time for reading and writing
-a reader and/or scribe if they are so slow at doing it on their own without support ... Or the level of spelling and writing skill is so poor that the answer is not understood ...
-Extra time for breaks if stress is a major issue, and they need to be able to use some stress relief and focusing techniques.

-Food provisions if blood sugar levels are important to their ability to stay focused throughout the task.

To be able to get these provisions you will need to have had medical reports from a developmental paediatric specialist and probably a specialist Speech Pathologist, who will be able to test the student to be able to write an appropriate report to be submitted to the Board of Studies.

Then the school will have to do their own test administration with the student. First without any assistance in a timed situation, then with extra time, reader or scribe—to be able to know the different results with and without assistance or provisions. This process can be quite stressful for the student, but it then gives a truer picture showing that there is ability and intelligence. They just need assistance to allow it to come through.

These steps are not necessary if their dyslexia has been corrected.

Has your son or any of your students ever received special provisions at school or after?

No, my son never did. Quite the opposite, the teachers at high school never believed me that he is dyslexic. He also never wanted to be or look different. From all of my students, I only know one who had a scribe for the bigger exams, as her range of difficulties was beyond most clients and her abilities and intelligence far outweighed her performance. As I am not an educational psychologist, I am not qualified to write a report that would be accepted by the Board of

Studies for special provisions. The testing we do is an initial assessment that determines if the person is suitable for the Davis program, what academic level they are currently at, how motivated they are to change and what their goals are. It gives them a great insight into their unique way of perceiving reality, what changes to expect from the program and how to go forward into and after a program.

What about a balanced brain?

Being balanced and able to use both the left to the right side of your brain is a great gift and one that can be developed. The new research in neuroscience, also supported by epi-genetics, as promoted by Dr. Bruce Lipton and many others, point to our ability to change our brain at any age. Epi-genetics literally means above genetics. Our mind can override the conditioning or the genetic disposition we inherited.

How to communicate successfully and support all family members who might have right-brain tendencies?

That is actually a very interesting question. Often communication can lead to misunderstandings with family members who think differently. Giving very long and detailed instructions of what you expect from someone who thinks in pictures is counter-productive, as most likely their mind will switch off after one minute and cancels out everything. Too many words lead some kids to simply "sign out," which you can tell when you watch their eyes. Some kids report to me that all they hear after a while is "blah-blah-blah." Same at school, when teachers are too "wordy" and don't interrupt monologues to ask questions or add activities. In communication, too, dyslexics are found somewhere outside the box. They are either very poor or excellent communicators ... but excellent communication skills don't always go hand in hand with excellent listening skills.

How do Asperger's and autism fit into the picture of right-brain thinking?

Children and adults on the Autistic Spectrum (AS) are also right-brain dominant, but in most other areas they show a completely different profile. Some are dyslexic as well, but not necessarily. While the dyslexic mindset has an overactive Mind's Eye (having the visual attention moving around, finding it difficult to focus on one area), autistic individuals usually disorient more auditory, so you could say the Mind's Ear is as busy as the Mind's Eye for dyslexics.

You often see these children in libraries or in quiet corners, trying to drone out the noises. Their sense of hearing is often so heightened, because they have an ability/problem to be in the sound, rather than perceiving it from the place where the body is. Imagine a noise coming from the lawn-mower outside the window, another from the ceiling fan, another from a talking neighbour, another from a toilet flashing next door, which could sound like a tsunami ... no wonder there is huge overwhelm.

Once out of alignment, other senses follow and are often also more heightened. Smells can become unbearable, touch is too much, emotion-overload, taste too much, etc.

How does Davis deal with autism? Don't they also have a Davis Autism Approach?

That is too big a question to answer in one paragraph, but there is a new book out by Abigail Marshall with Ronald D. Davis called *Autism and the Seeds of Change* and also a website, www.davisautism.com, that explains how very differently Ron views autism. Ron Davis, being autistic himself, has an amazing insight and unique approach to helping autistic individuals to fully participate in life.

Basically, the program's first aim is for people on the autistic spectrum to "individuate," which means giving their Mind's Ear that stable orientation to hear the sounds from the perspective of their body.

For non-verbal and severely autistic individuals, a specifically designed device is placed between the shoulder blades, functioning like a tiny radio, playing a special frequency sound that brings the focus back to the person. The device, designed by Ron Davis, is called a NOIT and I had the fortune of participating in their first trial run and the changes I have seen in non-verbal autistic children were astounding. At a later stage, concept work helps these children to make sense of our world in the third dimension, first personally, then in relationships to others.

The aim is not to "cure" autism, but to coax individuals into establishing a stable orientation. The sound places a person's attention to one area so often that it becomes the focal point of attention. It removes the chaos from the environment and once one sense has established a stable orientation, all others follow.

Again, Ron Davis does not believe that these individuals are broken or have a disease that needs a cure. He believes that inherent in them is the seed of a genius, a new paradigm for society.

Are dyslexia, ADD or ADHD the same thing or part of the same problem?

ADD or ADHD is not always associated with dyslexia, but very often they are an extension of it. Sometimes the food children eat (or the artificial additives and preservatives) cause hyperactivity in children, or aggravate the situation. Being a part of dyslexia, I treat it in exactly the same way—not as a disease or disability, but a need to create orientation to stabilize the sense of time, balance, motion— and with it regulate the output of dopamine. However, if a child is on Ritalin or another stimulant, we are not allowed to work with them until they have been off the drugs for about three weeks. After the program, there is no need to get back to the drug, if the exercises are continued.

Instead of a Dyslexia Correction Program, an Attention Mastery Program may be of benefit. ADD Programs focus less on reading issues and more on focus and concept work.

What causes ADD/ADHD?

ADD or Attention Deficit Disorder, means, according to the Merck Manual and the Psychiatric Association's Diagnostic Manual, a developmentally inappropriate inattention and impulsivity with and without hyperactivity. It is seen ten times more frequently in boys than in girls. ADD children aren't overly active; they may display restlessness or jitteriness, a short attention span, difficulty to finish a task or distractibility. ADHD children show additionally a difficulty to remain seated, an impulse to move.

Medical professionals may diagnose the symptoms but are unable to find the cause or address any underlying problems ... so Ritalin or another stimulant is often the answer from the medical establishment. What they cannot see or test, of course, is the underlying cause: disorientation. Just about any emotional high or low can cause disorientation, from being bored to feeling highly anxious or confused.

I don't believe that ADD is an appropriate term, as there certainly is NOT a lack of attention, often quite the opposite. Attention can be extremely high when absorbed in a computer game, a TV show or an area of interest. In a classroom setting, that attention can easily be scattered to many activities or stimuli. Instead of focused attention, the minds of ADD/ADHD children overindulge in a wide variety of distractions. Every shift of perception creates a spontaneous disorientation—and with it a shift of our perception of time. ADD children display higher levels of dopamine around the synapsis, speeding up their internal clock. The increased internal clock, the illusion of time outside being slower, is counterbalanced by a need to increase motion. I have seen it over and over again, that a correction of the disorientation causes a total shift in my client's perception and the signs of distractibility and hyperactivity disappear. A teacher who creates interest in his subject often has a huge impact on the level of hyperactivity in children.

What is hypoactivity?

Both hyperactivity and hypoactivity have the same root cause: disorientation, but at its effect, they show a reversal of perception of time. While for the hyperactive child the internal clock is speeding up and real time appears very slow in comparison, for the hypoactive child the opposite is true. The world outside seems to be too fast. They often disappear into their own reality and therefore also display a difficulty to stay on task. These kids appear to be lethargic, inactive, daydreamers, lazy or just not motivated.

Can dyslexia be a handicap if not corrected?

That is an excellent question, but the answer may vary from one dyslexic person to the next. Since there are no two individuals displaying the same show of symptoms, the variety of solutions is equally high. The dyslexic adults I see in my practice certainly have not "outgrown" their dyslexic tendencies or found an adequate solution; otherwise they wouldn't seek my help. They would certainly agree that the perceived handicap has to be corrected to stop influencing their lives in a negative way. Others have found "their niche" and successfully avoided having to perform in a profession that doesn't suit their big-picture mind. Richard Branson couldn't be called handicapped by his dyslexia, but being in his position, he wouldn't be required to delve into literacy, write letters himself or read his own legal documents. I have talked to many dyslexics who admitted to having made sure to be successful enough to be able to afford staff or at least a secretary to deal with the areas they'd be struggling with.

Does it only cause problems at school, because the system is left-brain oriented?

The school is not the only area with left-brain dominance. Many professional areas, where finer details, precision, order, efficiency or a chain of sequential and logical procedures are required, dyslexics could experience difficulties with. Any school system, that includes more of the right-brain, visual, large scale, global or a creative process, would benefit dyslexics. Even a more balanced approach is helpful, as the right-brain approach is ideal to start a project with, which then can lead to the left brain providing the detail, speed, efficiency and automaticity to complete and maintain it.

Many dyslexic adults find ways to compensate for weaknesses by partnering with people of left-brain strengths – privately and professionally. However, this is not unique to dyslexics. Most people are attracting opposites to complement their own qualities.

What can I tell my child to feel more confident about their dyslexia?

Depending on their age, using appropriate examples, explain the gift that their way of thinking comes with. My own passion about the abilities of that mindset probably helps, but all my clients end up being really proud of the fact that they are part of an elite club of people with a dyslexic learning style. Depending on their interest, I'd point out Walt Disney or Tom Cruise, Keira Knightley or Einstein, Leonardo da Vinci or Quentin Tarantino and just about any top sportsperson. All these people didn't succeed despite being dyslexic, but **because** of it. Most of these individuals did struggle at school, were teased or bullied, but once they found their strength and used their gifts, many of them went straight to the top of their field. In today's workplace, opportunities for dyslexics are greater than ever, not only because of our increased need for creative solutions but also our heavy dependence on the internet and technology, which really suits right brainers.

Can you tell me more about the associated anxiety that so often goes with dyslexia and mainstream schooling?

It is really not surprising that with our emphasis on academic achievements, anybody who does not hit the benchmark would feel anxious or inferior. Mainstream schooling has added another twist with our "No Child Left Behind" Policy that aims to improve the odds for underserved students. Although seemingly a logical approach that should benefit children who are struggling, it

184

unfortunately often achieves the opposite: a child feeling even less capable of being part of mainstream, feeling different or ostracized. I am sure there is a lot more to this topic—and that many children do feel happy with learning a trade, but many others are just not given a choice. Anything seems better than anxiety and struggle. Our society also fails to provide adequate support and education about stress-releasing non-invasive modalities that would highly benefit these children. Modalities like EFT (Emotional Freedom Technique), meditation, yoga, etc. would be very beneficial for all children, not only dyslexic ones. The sad fact that a children's version of Prozac has the most increased prescription of any drug in the USA, gives testimony to our failure to achieve a positive parenting and learning environment for our children.

Would dyslexic primary school children benefit from a Montessori-style schooling program?

I personally like the Montessori-style schooling, having seen a very positive result for my two older children who attended until the age of seven. They are both not dyslexic, but I also find the approach very much suited to the dyslexic mindset. Montessori promotes a hands-on approach, a "teach-me to do it myself" attitude that nurtures confidence and individuality, but also adds the structure necessary to build many study and life skills. I feel that also Rudolf Steiner schools/ Waldorf schools fall under this category. All of them discourage the boxing in of our children. Instead they foster a kinaesthetic approach to learning allowing them to grow at their own rate and in their area of strength.

Will they really be okay when they go to high school and find "their thing"?

This question actually suggests an anxious mother that might benefit from reading the book and relaxing. The thoughts, feelings and emotions of the family and the environment our children grow up in—be it a dyslexic or any other child—have a huge influence on the image they create of themselves. If you as a mother worry and fear, even if you don't openly show it, you are influencing the confidence of your child. They simply feel it, thinking there is something wrong with them.

Depending on how severely dyslexic a child is, an intervention is always a good thing, as long as the energy behind the help is one of positive, relaxed care. When dragging a child from one psychiatrist to another therapist, doctors, OTs, psychologists, specialists, speech therapists, etc. it is no wonder they cannot get the belief that they will be okay. I am not against getting an opinion or seeing any one of these therapists. The question should be: "How can I help my child to feel even more confident and happy?" (Instead of: "How come my child is not coping? Why is he struggling so much? What is wrong with my child?") Some children will naturally thrive in high school or at Uni, without much help, others won't. When they make it all the way to Uni, they usually have found "their thing" and will indeed thrive.

How do you keep their confidence and self-esteem up when they think they are less than others in class?

I have found that being told how clever they are doesn't hurt, but is not really believed either. "Of course, you'd say that; you are my mother," seems to be the most common reaction to the opinions of the family. Confidence has to be felt and earned, in order to be believed. In my profession as Davis facilitator, the building of confidence through self-mastery is my first goal. It follows the natural order from relaxation to focus; from focus to attention; from attention to achievement and from there to mastery. Self-esteem is a natural consequence of mastery and the most rewarding result for anyone to witness.

When you see a transformation from a nervy, anxious, timid child or teenager to a calm, self-assured and confident person, the benefits extend well beyond the classroom.

It influences the choice of their peer-group, which area of learning and living they focus on and what they consequently achieve in life. They will know that they are different, but definitely not less than others. Most of them end up being happy to be different.

As much as young people want to fit in and don't want to be perceived as different, we change and seek to stand out later in life.

At that point we are happy and confident to have a gift that is seen as different and valuable to other. Dyslexics can certainly provide that.

How do I continue supporting my child if they are not motivated to change or don't want to participate positively in a program?

Motivation is key! It does not matter where it comes from, but please try to find one area, even if it is outside of school that the child is motivated to make a change. Ask them casual questions to figure out, where they are at, who they hang out with, what they love and what they don't like. Ask them why that is so. Ask them if they would like to feel less stressed out at school, or if they want to make reading or writing easier for themselves? If the answer to all of them is negative, and they don't want to change at all, it is often better to wait until they do. Otherwise the pushing will only end in struggle and frustration.

Some children prefer to be left alone to pursue their art, sport or other area they are good at and happy to indulge in. As long as these hobbies are not negatively influencing their health and wellbeing, it might be great to encourage and join them in those activities and ease up on the rest. You will be surprised how often they will make a huge shift, as soon as they feel that the pressure from you is gone.

One day this child of yours will surprise you! Trust them, they come with their own "instruction manual" and might just take another route to their destination than you'd like them to take. If, however, your child wants help in one area of their life, don't sabotage it by trying to persuade them to go into another area or an additional one.

It has to be their choice and their responsibility—as the outcome is their life and the mastery of it.

Are there other strategies that I have as a mum to support my child, apart from supporting her interests, e.g., in art, or discussing things with her?

Unconditional love is a good strategy to apply. It is, however, best to start with yourself. Unless you are happy, how can your girl benefit or learn to be happy. If you love art, do it for **you**. Your passion will create a wonderful emotional link with your child. But if your child loves art and you love yoga, each should be happy and free to delve into their own hobby.

Discussion is great, especially if it involves questions and listening to the answers. Many mums believe that discussions are there to convince a child of her own point of view. Although the motives are always pure and in the best interest of the child, the outcome is disempowerment. Questions help a child best to discover answers and feel empowered; they will end up owning the changes when they are ready to walk that path.

When my dyslexic son entered Year 7, I stopped checking his homework and did not look at it for the following six years unless he gave me an essay to look at, which might have been once a year. Was his spelling or grammar perfect? Of course not. But as far as I heard from his teachers, he never failed to put in his homework and continued to get better every year. He had taken on full responsibility

189

for his own learning, which is only possible if mum fully releases it.

I have a dyslexic friend who is the CEO of one of the most successful publicity companies. He needs help writing letters etc.
What are the right measures of ability for young people with dyslexia that can indicate and encourage their ability despite their very basic challenges with writing and reading abilities? If not handled correctly, isn't there a lot of room for psychological harm?

Yes, I believe that we can potentially harm any child, psychologically or otherwise—by making them feel less worthy, by judging them, ridiculing them, disempowering them or by any other means. Dyslexic children may be more misunderstood and mistreated in a school setting, but a lack of awareness does not apply to them exclusively.

Naturally it will be far more beneficial to encourage their abilities, but that requires a deeper understanding of the mindset of dyslexia. In an effort to improve their students, some educators attempt well-meaning, but misguided discipline to instil what they perceive as lacking or defect. They misinterpret their mixed results as laziness, failing to see how much harder these students work as the rest of the class. Some teachers are open-minded and supportive and have a positive influence on bringing forth the gifts of these visual learners.

My son's teacher doesn't believe he is dyslexic. She thinks he has problems with his "working memory." What does that mean?

Working memory is usually measured by holding a limited amount of words/information in mind for a short period of time. As these tests commonly use letters or numbers, which is confusing and rather meaningless for picture-thinkers, dyslexics often rate very poorly in such tests. Sequence is another area of difficulty for them, so it is not really the working memory that is a problem, but the means of testing. If however the letters or numbers were replaced with real-life objects and if your son is dyslexic (or a picture thinker), then he'd rate very strongly in the area of working memory.

If your son is old enough, approximately eight years or over, there is a simple test to give you a rough idea. If your son is dyslexic, he will most likely think in images. Ask him to create a movie in his head, the complexity of which depends on the age of your son. I usually tell them a story, on how I get to work, asking them to follow my story in their mind.

E.g., I am driving my car into the parking station, where I leave my car, while I am working (make the first picture of the parking lot, what I'd see when I step out of my car), I then have to walk across a lovely green park, where I cross a Japanese-type bridge (make a second picture from the top of the bridge). After that I enter the tall building, where my office is. I press the button to the lift, when the lift door opens, take the third picture. I ride up to the first floor, get out of the lift and see a big square hallway with a peaceful looking Buddha statue (make that the fourth picture). I open the door and hang up my coat in a wardrobe (make the inside of the wardrobe your fifth image). I go up to the reception and greet the secretary (make the reception the sixth picture). The view behind her desk is stunning. Through the window I see the ocean, with big waves (seventh picture). I walk upstairs to my studio (the eight stairs are the eighth picture). I have a big whiteboard in my studio and write something on it (whiteboard is ninth picture). Then I tell them where they sit down on the big wooden desk, there is a lovely big pot-plant next to it. The tenth and last picture is of the pot-plant. Of course pause between the pictures as this takes time to process.

These very complex instructions are usually quite easy for a dyslexic mindset to follow and repeat afterwards. They are great visual aids to pin memories to. If, for example, they had to remember a list of things in the right sequence, this will help greatly.

It could be as simple as remembering mum's shopping list: 1. milk (see milk spilled on the floor of the parking lot/pic 1); 2. Toast (throw crumbs of bread to the fish over the bridge in the park, pic 2); 3. Sausages (see sausages hanging from the ceiling of the lift, pic 3); 4. Cheese (see the Buddha in the hallway holding a big round cheese); 5. Salad (see big salad heads tumbling out of the wardrobe, pic 5); 6. Carrots (see your secretary eating a carrot, pic 6); 7. Oranges (see oranges floating on the waves in the ocean, pic 7); 8. Apples (see an apple on each of the 8 steps, pic 8); 9. Fish (see me draw a fish on the whiteboard, pic 9); 10: tea (see tea bags hanging off the pot-plant, pic 10).

The funnier the images, the better the memory. There are no wrong ways and the original story can be anything the child can relate to, including their morning routine on the way to school etc.

Even if they only remember six or seven of the ten, it's a good working memory, believe me! I worked with a lovely nine-year-old girl last week, who was apparently struggling with working memory. I asked her to describe her way to school and pause, whenever I asked her to take a picture of the "freeze frame." She ended up with ten gorgeous images (garage at home, church across the schoolyard, steps, locker, door, whiteboard, desk, lunchbox, lunch shelter and handball).

She not only recalled all ten "stations" without a problem, but could name the entire shopping list, that I had asked her to integrate into the images, three hours later, when mum picked her up. Mum and I were amazed. So much for a poor working memory!

I have learnt a lot from a guy called Jim Kwik. He stated that there is no such thing as a good or a bad memory, just a trained or untrained one. Unfortunately our schools are only telling us what to learn and not how to.

It is therefore up to us to teach our children how to improve their focus and how to use their minds and bring them into the new age of learning – where they know how to apply their unique talents to remember and recall all the information they need.

How can you tell if a child is oriented and using the tools they get during a program—or in a state of disorientation?

I always tell my clients that their tools are invisible—and there is no way I can see an orientation point. But, I can still see if they are oriented or not—by one simple effect:

A person's balance. We always fall in the direction of the mind; that means where the attention currently rests. Of course this is not our conscious choice but usually a subconscious coping strategy.

While the client stands on one leg (knee gently bent and foot facing backwards or forward and alternating between legs for comfort), without wobbling, the mind has found the "spot." Wherever the body sways or falls to shows me the area where the mind is hovering at that moment.

We use that state of balance to add a ball exercise, that is aimed to help stabilize the new orientation, helps coordination, can solve a possible left-right confusion, and by catching the balls on either side of the head, the new neural pathways get reinforced. I am tossing these rubbery stringy balls at them, underhanded and they catch them with either hand without losing balance. These so called Koosh balls can be thrown backwards and forward between two or more people. Every time the person reaches over to catch, they are crossing the midline and their brain creates a neural pathway between the left and the right hemisphere.

After all, the aim is to create a balanced brain, where the creative and

194

intuitive gifts of the right-brained dominance is still active and nurtured, while at the same time, the left hemisphere (our logical, sequential and structured part of the brain) is getting fully awakened and integrated.

There is nothing more powerful than a whole-brain-approach (not a hole-in-the-brain).

What else can help these children once they get new tools to learn?

Of course **using** the tools is vital, as well as the new ways of reading, the above mentioned ball exercises and mastering the trigger words. Additionally, I have found it most useful to make sure that they eat well, exercise and have a healthy emotional environment.

These qualities of life are not unique to dyslexics, but being as sensitive as most of them are, they tend to react rather overwhelmed when in stressful situations. What looks like a dramatic overreaction to most of us, can actually be an indication of what their mind is going through.

I have seen many drama queens and although it's usually best to ignore the show; it also gives a fair picture of the state they are in.

Recommended Reading

All Cats have Asperger Syndrome (Kathy Hoopmann)
All Dogs have ADHD (Kathy Hoopmann)
Attention Deficit Disorder: A Different Perspective (T. Hartmann)
Autism and the Seeds of Change (Abigail Marshall with Ronald D. Davis)
Barron's Mathematics Study Dictionary (Frank Tapson)
Children: The Challenge (Rudolf Dreikurs, M.D.)
Creative Visualization (Shakti Gawain)
Disconnected Kids (Robert Melillo)
Exploring Time (Gillian Chapman & Pam Robson)
Getting the Horse to Drink (Suzanne H. Stevens)
If you want to be Rich and Happy, don't go to School (Robert Kiyosaki)
In the Mind's Eye (Thomas G. West)
Kids beyond Limits (Anat Baniel)
Learning how to Learn (Joyanne Cobb)
Learning outside the Line (Jonathan Mooney)
Life Visioning (Michael Beckwith)
Math at Hand (Great Source Education Group)
My stroke of Insight (Jill Bolte Taylor)
Overcoming Dyslexia (Sally Shaywitz, M.D.)
Raising Boys (Steve Biddulph)
Right-Brained Children in a Left-Brained World: Unlocking the Potential of your ADD Child (Jeffrey Freed & Laurie Parsons)
Smart but Stuck (Myrna Orenstein, Ph.D.)
Strong-Willed Child or Dreamer? (Dana Spears & Ron Braund)
The ADD Myth (Martha Burge)
The Biology of Belief (Bruce H. Lipton, Ph.D.)
The Brain that Changes Itself (Norman Doidge)

The Everything Parent's Guide to Children with Dyslexia (Abigail Marshall)
The Gift of Dyslexia (Ronald D. Davis)
The Gift of Learning (Ronald D. Davis)
The Hate to Write But Have to Writer's Guide (Jim Evers)
The Horse Boy (Rupert Isaacson)
The Macmillan Visual Dictionary (Jean-Claude Corbell)
The Myth of the ADD Child: 50 Ways to improve your Child's Behaviour and Attention Span without Drugs, Labels or Coercion (Thomas Armstrong, Ph.D.)
The Right Mind: Making Sense of the Hemispheres (Robert Ornstein)
The Secret Life of the Dyslexic Child (Robert Frank, Ph.D.)
Uniquely Gifted: Identifying and Meeting the Needs of the Twice-Exceptional Student (ed. Kiesa Kay)
Upside-Down Brilliance: The Visual-Spatial Learner (Linda Kreger Silverman, Ph.D.)
Webster's New World Children's Dictionary (The New York Press)
What in the World is a Homophone? (Leslie Presson)
You Don't Have to be Dyslexic (Dr. Joan Smith)
Your Child's Growing Mind (Dr. Jane Healy)

6052815R00115

Printed in Great Britain
by Amazon.co.uk, Ltd.,
Marston Gate.